Jules Sturm
Bodies We Fail

Jules Sturm (PhD) is assistant professor of Literary Studies and Cultural Analysis at the University of Amsterdam. His research interests are critical theories of the body in the fields of queer and disability studies, and posthuman theories.

Jules Sturm

Bodies We Fail

Productive Embodiments of Imperfection

[transcript]

Bibliographic information published by the Deutsche Nationalbibliothek
The Deutsche Nationalbibliothek lists this publication in the Deutsche Natio-
nalbibliografie; detailed bibliographic data are available in the Internet at
http://dnb.d-nb.de

© 2014 transcript Verlag, Bielefeld

Cover layout: Kordula Röckenhaus, Bielefeld
Cover illustration: Antony Crossfield, London, »Narcissus«
    (from the series »Foreign Body«), 2008, courtesy of the artist,
    Klompching Gallery (New York) & MiTO Gallery (Barcelona)
Edited, Proofread, and Typeset by Jim Gibbons, New York
Printed by Majuskel Medienproduktion GmbH, Wetzlar
Print-ISBN 978-3-8376-2609-4
PDF-ISBN 978-3-8394-2609-8

Für Heinze

Contents

Illustrations

Acknowledgments

This book emerged from my PhD project, which I conducted over the past years and successfully concluded in 2012 at the Amsterdam School for Cultural Analysis (ASCA), University of Amsterdam. The making of this book has been shaped by innumerable encounters, not only with numerous books, theories, thoughts, embodiments, art works, sights, and talks, but also with people. I want to acknowledge those who were indispensible for this project.

I express my deepest gratitude to my PhD supervisors Mieke Bal, Hanneke Grootenboer, and Murat Aydemir. While writing my MA thesis, I read Mieke's Introduction to *The Practice of Cultural Analysis* (1999), and I felt that research has, after all, something to offer me, and moreover, that it has the potential to change the world; a belief that I had almost given up and that came back with a force that has not left me ever since. When I met Mieke in person and was invited to participate in her Theory Seminar before I even started my PhD, I was convinced that the most critical and constructive of academic worlds was being built right then and there, at ASCA: a world that allowed for the simultaneous existence of oppositional standpoints, that translated conflicting disciplinary languages and traditions into inclusive conceptual thoughts, and that productively dealt with the potential failure of such translations. Mieke not only inspired this world with her own brilliance and generosity, but she also encouraged other bright minds to join: Hanneke and Murat have not only shared the small triumphs when one chapter after the other finally took shape, but they also suffered with me through periods of struggle and doubt about my writing and thinking. Their theoretical expertise, close reading, and patience were as valuable to this project as their sympathetic and unobtrusive insistence on probing my borders. Finally, Mieke's, Hanneke's, and Murat's kindness and spirit of companionship made this project truly pleasurable and finally led to the publication of this book.

I want to thank ASCA for hosting my dissertation, for being the source of intellectual inspiration and social exchange, for supporting me in practical, financial, as well as administrative matters, and for serving as my scholarly home base. My heartfelt thanks go to Eloe Kingma, Ania Dalecki, and Jantine van Gogh for their positive and matter-of-factly way of dealing with the most intricate problems of the lives of PhD candidates and young researchers.

I am obliged to Ruth Sonderegger, Maaike Bleeker, Jaap Kooijman, Patricia Pisters, and Kati Röttger for kindly accepting to be on my promotion committee. They made the commonly dreaded oral defense procedure a pleasurable and inspiring event.

I wish to express my gratitude to the *Koninklijke Nederlandse Akademie van Wetenschappen* (KNAW) for the doctoral fellowship that made this PhD financially possible.

For their diligence and eye for details in editing my manuscript, I am grateful to Murat Aydemir and Jim Gibbons. Jim, a special thanks to you for dealing so elegantly and calmly with the unexpected difficulties we both encountered in adapting different publication formats across countries and languages. For her support in developing my writing skills, her enthusiasm and optimism despite hard times, I want to thank Susan Stocker. For advocating my work and publishing an early version of one of my chapters in *Disturbing Bodies* (2008), I am indebted to Sylvia Mieszkowski. I am grateful to the artists Anthony Crossfield, Del LaGrace Volcano, Gitta Gsell, and Marc Quinn to so generously allow me to publish their work free of charge. The creative and very personal exchange I had with Anthony and Del was a deeply enriching experience.

I am grateful to my friends and colleagues at the University of Amsterdam for their creative input, shared struggles, as well as regular vital distractions from work: Hanneke Stuit, Daan Wesselman, Boris Noordenbos, Astrid Van Weyenberg, Anik Fournier, and Pepita Hesselberth. My dearest colleague, faithful office mate, and wonderful friend Noa Roei saved me from more than one breakdown in the process of publishing this book. Noa, you are truly my best partner; I am hoping for many more serious, supportive, insightful encounters between the two of us in the coming years. For the invitation to and the collaboration at lectures, conferences, and other thought-inspiring events in Vienna, Hamburg, Berlin, Basel, Zurich, and Amsterdam I wish to thank my dear friends Sushila Mesquita, Skadi Loist, and Si-Phi Kutzenberger.

Mireille, thank you for always being there, exchanging thoughts, listening, and saying just the right things at the right times. You are my most precious reminder of how vulnerable, painful, yet desirable our shared lives are. Sonja, how can I thank you enough for never questioning our old bond of friendship despite your legitimate reservations about my thoughts and beliefs? Sophie, throughout the past years, you were my knight in shining armor, rescuing me from "totttalll disasterrrs" with your wit, courage, faithfulness, and relentless vigor.

Finally, I want to thank my family: Mum, for your unwavering love and commitment, despite your skepticism. Pa, for your warmth, care, and encouragement; your skills in formatting typescripts are really fabulous. Dominic, for being the best of big brothers, my oldest companion, and the most serious interlocutor, challenger, and defender of my quirks. Bri, my favorite cousin, for your infinite energy and persistence in supporting my life and my work.

Heinze, for thirteen years of shared love, life, and work: you are and have been the most valuable source of inspiration, motivation, and humor throughout all these years of writing. When my work took its toll on my sanity, you found the strength to keep believing in me. For your dedication in every respect, I dedicate this book to you – *with all my heart.*

Arthur, fröhliches Wesen, thank you for materializing so miraculously in our life.

Introduction

Ästhetik ist ja nichts als eine angewandte Physiologie.

FRIEDRICH NIETZSCHE

All art comes from terrific failures and terrific needs that we have. It is about the difficulty of being a self because one is neglected. Everywhere in the modern world there is neglect, the need to be recognized, which is not satisfied. Art is a way to recognize oneself.

LOUISE BOURGEOIS

The queer art of failure turns on the impossible, the improbable, the unlikely, and the unremarkable. It quietly loses, and in losing it imagines other goals for life, for love, for art, and for being.

JUDITH HALBERSTAM

In August 2010, I visited an exhibition of the artists Louise Bourgeois and Hans Bellmer in Berlin.[1] In juxtaposing a selection of works by these two

---

1 *Double Sexus* was shown at Sammlung Scharf-Gerstenberg, Berlin, in summer 2010. The exhibition was later shown at Gemeente Museum in The Hague in winter 2010-11.

artists, *Double Sexus* created an intimate dialogue between two surrealists who never met. At the center of this dialogue stood the question of the human body. The exhibition's title alludes to the insoluble form of the sexes, which was represented in the show by manifestations of androgyny, duplicated limbs, and mirrored sexual organs. In unapologetic defiance of the identifiable body, the exhibition staged encounters with an abundance of unusual embodiments, challenging with humor and creativity our abiding beliefs in corporeal norms.

As presented in *Double Sexus*, the artists' works portray the body as a boundless life-form that both allows and extends our forms of perception. In contrast to presentations of the human body as an object, often suggesting an inflexible nature, here it is represented as a variable in social, sexual, and political life. Moreover, the body is treated as a form of critical art, which blurs the boundaries between artist and art object, self and other, sameness and difference, norm and deviation. In these respects, *Double Sexus* is exemplary for the book that is to follow.

THE BODY IN ART

"For me," observes Bourgeois, "sculpture is the body. My body is sculpture" (Kittelmann and Zacharias 2010). Of course, such a focus on the body has had a long and varied history, going back at least to the late 1950s, when the term "body art" was coined and began its evolution.[2] Associated with artists such as Bruce Nauman, Gilbert and George, Otto Mühl, Hermann Nitsch, Carolee Schneemann, and Vito Acconci, it grew to encompass the works of Marina Abramovic, Hannah Wilke, and VALIE EXPORT, among others. Body art was above all an activist art form, reflecting a new experience of subjectivity that was embodied rather than transcendental: it was necessarily contingent on others, and irreducible to a single image. The genre intersected with the student protests of the 1960s and 70s and the liberationist discourses of movements advocating greater rights and freedoms for women and for gays and lesbians. It assumed the use or enactment of the artist's body in the work of art. In opposition to

---

2   On the history of body art and further developments in body-oriented art practices, see Jones 1998.

Cartesian thought, which postulates a mind-body split and assumes knowledge to be stable and objective, body artists reconceived the subject as being simultaneously non-coherent and embodied. The body was thus recognized as a central actor to challenge conventions of subjecthood.

Whereas earlier body artists focused mainly on the body's role in self-other relationships, the artists who came later tended to explore the body *as* self and to expose it as unnatural, or what some have called "posthuman."[3] Body-oriented art practices of the late twentieth century, by artists such as Orlan, Laura Aguilar, and Stelarc, treated the body as an organic and indeed mortal organism, whose corporeality was mutable. These artists refused the conception of a fixed materiality. By turning the body inside out, they claimed visual representation to be (at least partially) unsuccessful in comprehending the meaning of "self." Subjectivity was exposed as something that could not be grasped, even with the help of technological mediation, abstract knowledge, or through the flesh itself, because it failed to show itself in a recognizable, visible form.

This "loss" of the self, and the simultaneous transmutability of the body, is also the focal point of the art of Bourgeois and Bellmer. Yet, in my view, and in apparent contrast with many body artists, they treat the body not as magical nut to crack or foreign planet to explore, but as intimate companion to love and cherish. The body invites this relationship because of its emblematic negativity, its vulnerability, its deficient stability, and, last but not least, its mortality. Their art involves the body as emotional object, which thus enters the world of a self that *feels* rather than *knows* or acknowledges the limit of knowledge. By incorporating the possibility of failure into projects related to physicality and humanity, the two artists not only expose the body's limitations, but they extend the body's dimensions.

---

3   "Posthuman" is a term used in critical theory to describe the reconsideration of the "historically specific construction called *the human*" (Hayles 1999: 2). The posthuman view, the body as biological substrate for the human being is questioned; instead, the body is postulated as a prosthesis of human consciousness that we have learned to manipulate, and the embodied human is seen as being seamlessly entwined with intelligent machines. By regarding the biological body as a questionable basis for the human, the assumption that a "self" resides in this body becomes problematic as well. For more on the history of the posthuman, see Hayles 1999.

This embrace of seemingly negative corporeal attributes, which most expressions of body art have sought to overcome, is of central importance to my project. In this study, I analyze works of literature, dance performance, photography, and sculpture that are representative of body art practices in that they "place the body/self within the realm of the aesthetic *as a political domain*" (Jones 1998: 13). This aesthetic proposes that art is not only a means to disrupt hegemonic body politics, but is also a site where corporeal or sensory perception is negotiated. While I do not want to disregard the political aspects of body art practices in this book, I am primarily attempting to reconsider the "simple" practices of reading and seeing corporeality. These cultural practices are analyzed and challenged by looking at ambiguous, disabled, partially absent, doubled, or compounded bodies in specific cultural objects. Much in Bourgeois's sense, I aim to look at the body through its negative, disruptive, disabled, yet productively critical and indeed desirable characteristics.

The objects of my analysis in this book embody and expose these characteristics in different ways. In Djuna Barnes's novel *Nightwood*, the human body is presented as hovering precariously close to monstrous and animalistic realms of embodiment. The documentary film *augenblicke N* shows disabled bodies as exposing blindness toward difference. Claude Cahun, Del LaGrace Volcano, and Robert Mapplethorpe present photographic self-portraiture as a form of self-loss and bodily absence in representation. Finally, Antony Crossfield's and Robert Gober's artworks reveal that the progressive discourse of self-formation and the stable body-image is disabling for the development of aging identities. To analyze these particular cultural objects, I look at them through the lens of theoretical concepts that reflect a comparable historical or epistemic negativity. Marginalized fields of research in the humanities, such as queer, disability, and aging studies, have allowed me to address specific critical issues in the study of the body. Simultaneously, I use the sensory quality of the artworks to highlight the shortcomings of disembodied and abstract forms of theory.

If bodies in art have triggered the awareness that bodies are products as well as agents of culture and social interaction rather than passive natural givens, bodies in theory have often been treated as the material, inert counterpoint to thought. Despite or because of their status as mere *objects* of analysis, bodies were banished from the process of knowledge production and were put on stage for theoretical inspection. The voyeuristic and disembodied character of many theories of the body causes something essential to be overlooked: namely, the "being there" of the theorist's body that perceives, senses, and feels what it observes and describes. This as-yet-disembodied practice of theory has motivated me to focus on cultural objects that have touched me, and thus have affected my theorizing. As a result, the body in art became linked to the body in theory in this study, adding to it a partly unseizable, mutable, yet material dimension.

THE BODY IN THEORY

Despite the body's absence or dismissal within dominant Western intellectual traditions, the familiar model of incorporeal abstraction became a contested site in theories of the mid-to-late twentieth century. In the wake of Descartes' rationalism, the body was rejected as an obstacle to rational knowledge production, resulting in a veritable somatophobia in the humanities (Robinson 2000: 72). The body was, however, never wholly absent from theory, and it played a key role in the development of theoretical methodologies; it was theorized in order to be transcended, in the pursuit of a fully rational subjectivity.[4]

The influence of phenomenological and psychoanalytic thought transformed such accounts of subjectivity by postulating an intricate and irreducible connection between the constitution of the subject and the body. Although sometimes accused of being indifferent to materiality, postmodern and poststructuralist theories radically changed the ways that bodies were theorized. The insight that the body is a discursive construction does not deny the material foundation of bodies, but it insists that an analysis of the body is necessarily mediated by the context in which it is conceived.[5]

However, despite the efforts to theorize the body, critical thinkers such as Jacques Lacan, Maurice Merleau-Ponty, Donna Haraway, and Judith Butler have made it increasingly clear that, as Gayatri Spivak asserts, "The

---

4   For turn-of-the-twentieth-century thought on physiognomy, see Sekula 1986.

5   In *Bodies That Matter* (1993), Judith Butler not only proposes the discursive construction of bodies but also, in reference to Derrida, conceptualizes the materialization of corporeal norms in and through language.

body, as such, cannot be thought" (Spivak, quoted in Butler 1993: 1). Yet, unlike their somatophobic predecessors, these theorists have regarded the body as multiple, unruly, and fathomless – embodying an infinity of differences in sexuality, skin color, class, age, ability, and mobility. This premise resonated with the longstanding nightmarish conceptions of the body as monstrous, leaky, contagious, and mysterious in mainstream cultural beliefs and practices. The categorizations of the human body as negative or unacceptable were now seen to be expressions of the body's productivity and unforeseeable promises. The simultaneous positive and negative interpretations of the same assumption – the uncontainable body – make the body not only a welcome object of study, but also a minefield of cultural contestation. Despite this development and the ensuing expansion of the body's definition, theory was forced to confront, and must continue to deal with, the material conditions of the body and the cultural regimes that surround and constitute it.

The body is a physical object in the sense that it exists in space and in time. Despite enduring continuous changes, and despite being an animated object, it maintains a certain form, is caught within specific boundaries, and ceases to exist as social body with the death of the person who inhabits it. The body is distinguished from other physical objects, or from the bodies of others, because the subject who inhabits it cannot get away from it, is able to view it only from certain perspectives or with the help of mirrors, and experiences kinesthetic and other sense perceptions – indeed, the world itself – only through that particular body. In addition to having this phenomenal self-experiential quality, the body, however, is an object that is significantly exposed to defining historical, geographical, and cultural conditions. Consequently, the body is at once a subject's most intimate experience, and her or his most inescapable form of public constitution.

The reason why a person can see her body only from certain perspectives is because one can only see with and through one's own body. [6] Theorists in gender and disability studies, phenomenology, psychoanalytic theory, performance studies, queer and visual theory have sought to incorporate this "seeing with." The body's duplicitous status as

---

6   Throughout this book, I will use a universal "she" rather than specifying two genders. This choice reflects the unfortunate yet recognizable limitation of gender pronouns in a world in which a multitude of gendered identities and bodies exist.

object and subject has probably been its most valuable characteristic in relation to theories of the body. However, despite its seemingly holistic nature, the body's most limiting yet constitutional companion is its blindness towards itself. The eyes with which a body sees the world and other bodies cannot see themselves seeing.

In this book I attempt to take the body's lack of self-seeing, which many theories of the body have contested and sought to overcome, as a productive quality, to be used to reveal new forms of "seeing," perceiving, or knowing. Instead of attempting to conquer this structural deficiency, I explore the possibilities of other forms of awareness, necessitated or enabled through limitation. I suggest that through a positive conception of certain restrictions of the self and the body – which have, negatively, been ascribed to culturally or physically marginalized groups and individuals – a theory of the body can become a tool to scrutinize unilateral tendencies toward positivism, strength, growth, performance, efficacy, efficiency, and a general dismissal of limitations.[7] The aspect of blindness or imperfect seeing not only promotes a theoretical dialogue with impaired, queer, colored, aged, or other culturally, socially, and politically restricted bodies, but it also calls for a cultural theory that accounts for the unacceptable aspects of every body. Advances in body augmentation or enhancement through the use of technology, medical developments, and the refusal to succumb to the human organism's circumstantial expiration: these developments have made it increasingly more difficult to theorize the body in its particular capacity to simultaneously represent objecthood and subjecthood, stability and change, conformity and individualism. My aim is not to develop an all-inclusive theory of the body, but to try to let the body in art be a mirror for theoretical accounts – accounts that ideally attempt to draw on their own blind spots to develop new forms of seeing and knowing.

THE "FAILING" BODY

Throughout this book I explore the effects of what I term "productive failure." Failure is a form of deficiency when an anticipated action is not

---

7   See a critical account of performance paradigms in McKenzie 2001.

achieved, or is accomplished in a different way than anticipated. Failure also signifies an inability to meet and conform to certain norms. These two most common definitions of failure are negatively connoted and depend on forms of achievement that assume and promote functionality, structural sameness, efficiency, positivity, evolution, and progress. As such, I find the effects of failure not particularly productive for critical thought, since they can only be measured in dichotomous terms such as good and bad, or better and worse.

To formulate another conception of failure, I want to refer to Kaja Silverman's paradigm of the "good enough" (1996: 4).[8] Silverman develops the notion of the "good enough" to dismantle the binary opposition between corporeal ideality and abjection. She thereby reveals that we can always only approximate an ideal even as we never totally fail to achieve a certain rendition of some ideals. In this sense, the "good enough" allows us to reeducate the look we direct toward our own and others' bodies by rejecting corporeal ideals and by giving more positive weight to physical approximation, partiality, difference, uncertainty, indeterminacy, improvisation, and "unreality" (ibid: 55). In Silverman's view, to fail to realize the ideal is to achieve the "possibility of productive vision – of an eye capable of seeing something other than what is given to be seen, and over which the self does not hold absolute sway" (ibid: 227). Failure is here expressed as producing something new and other, through a partial loss of control for the autonomous subject. Productive vision is thus built not only on failing ideality, but also on failing the self-sufficient and homogeneous subject. I take this critical yet productive version of "failure" as my starting point to argue for the positive transformative effects of other seemingly negative concepts surrounding the body, such as monstrosity, vulnerability, self-loss, absence, and aging.

---

8   Silverman borrows and develops her notion of the "good enough" from D. W. Winnicott's conception of the "good enough mother," who is "to be preferred to her ideal counterpart, since she does not attempt to fill the void upon which desire is predicated" (Silverman 1996: 225). Since every ideal is constituted on a projection, predication, or the expectation of others, which is not necessarily to the advantage of the child, the "good enough mother," and Silverman's more general adaptation of the "good enough" concept, breaks with the idea that our most productive forms are those of success, sufficiency, and fulfillment.

These concepts do not merely describe the failure of certain bodies to fulfill corporeal standards, but they also bring to the fore how these standards, and the culture at large, *fail* certain bodies and subjects; how failed bodies become failed selves and failed humans, and how they become outsiders, queers, and monsters. By reframing notions of corporeal failure, and by revealing the failure of vision and visibility, I aim to expose the deceptively all-encompassing bodily mappings of the human subject as exclusionary and prejudiced.[9] In this study, I claim that "failed bodies" are a valuable source for reeducating the ways we picture our bodies and our selves.

In chapter 1, I use the negatively connoted concept of the monster as a means of corruption; with the monster figure I aim to corrupt the meaning of normal bodies. The concept of the monstrous body further allows me to reconsider how bodies are commonly read and interpreted. The monster embodies a plurality of differences and challenges categories of humanity, race, age, sexuality, gender, and the subject, categories that are intrinsically linked to corporeality. Although the figure of the monster has long been a familiar and welcome subject in popular culture, it is in its role as a concept – the monstrous – that it is most disruptive. The monstrous body reflects both the creepy yet desired figure of the monster, as well as the unsettling concept of the monstrous, discomfiting because it remains ultimately strange and unknowable. Acknowledging that the monstrous is thus associated with otherness and exteriority, this chapter aims to read the traits of the monster that are beyond the projection of monstrosity onto the other. The monster is read as a productive form of embodiment, which motivates not only fear and disgust, but also desire and intimacy, and which gives an account of our culture's conception of human bodies. This chapter opens the stage for a discussion of other so-called negative concepts of the body.

In chapter 2, I use the concept of vulnerability, an existential state that may potentially belong to all bodies but has nonetheless been characterized

---

9   In her remarkable study on the queer art of failure, Judith Halberstam refers to Californian artist Judie Bamber to show how failures of visuality create a horizon of simultaneous possibility and disappointment. Halberstam contends that the subject of Bamber's is limitation and that the function of the limit in visibility means that we should learn to "adjust to less light rather than seek out more" (97; 105-6).

as a negative attribute. Like the notion of the monstrous, it is commonly projected onto others. However, I look at vulnerability from the perspective of subjects who use their experience of their bodies as vulnerable to reveal the shared vulnerability of looking and being looked at in the setting of the theatre. The critical contention of visuality and aesthetic paradigms around the body introduces a model for critical analysis of the subject's relation to image-making. This chapter looks at how the absence of corporeal strength and resistance might allow us to conceptualize a new aesthetic that would account for the frailty of vision. And this leads right into chapter 3, in which I analyze subject formations and the potential for gain in the loss of self.

Since the beginning of psychoanalytic theory, the formation of the self has been strongly linked to visual experience and the infant's encounter with its mirror image. The self and the body-image, formed in a shared process, are inseparable from the exception of what has been culturally termed a psychological or physical disorder. My analysis introduces the idea of self-loss as a way to disrupt the conception of a coherent alignment of self and body, which delimits the formation of a multiplicity of ever-transforming selves and varied body images. I use the concept of loss of self to point to the potential deficit of certain identificatory and visual categories. As such, the concept promises gain through loss and leads to chapter 4, in which I introduce the concept of absence as a means to look at those aspects of bodies that, though seeming to be invisible, are nonetheless decisive in a subject's bodily experience.

The blind spots that are generated by cultural constructions such as race, gender, or age here serve a double function: I use them to expose the projection of bodily markers onto others as a substitute for the self's search for recognition. And I propose that what is not recognizable about certain bodies gives them the particular potential to overcome or diffuse the frames of bodily representation. The image of a body, created by the beholder of another body, reflects the absence of the "real" body, yet too often represents the existence of a subject caught in the absorption of the look of the other. The pictured body and the living body are disparate but are mutually dependent for the development of the self; the body is understood as an image that mirrors a likeness with the surrounding world, not with a human embodiment that is inherent and fixed. As much as the mirror reflects the self and evokes the body-image, it does not contain the living body, which, in contrast to the framed image, grows, moves, and ages. On this basis, chapter 5 focuses on the delimiting function of the mirror for an embodied subject and on the consequential difficulty in conceiving of an aged body-image.

In my last chapter, I introduce the notion of aging, not only as a procedural and potentially productive characteristic of all bodies, but also as a concept to reveal and question the currently popular decline-value of Lacan's model of subject formation. I consider the idea of a reversed mirror-stage, which might do more justice to those bodies that, with age, outgrow the framed mirror and present us with alternative and more inclusive perspectives on the relation between bodies and selves.

Double Sexus's seductive yet challenging artistic exploration of the human body and self exemplifies my ambitions for this book, which are motivated by a similarly seductive quest for theories that might account for our *failure* of knowing or thinking our bodies. This quest is as much guided by my fascination with theories of the body as by critical and queer artworks, which not only show us the body's limitations, but also, and foremost, the limitations of cultural discourse, language, and visuality to express or grasp our bodies' variation, creativity, aliveness, and sensuality. Much in Bourgeois's spirit, I am guided here by the conviction that art as well as critical theory means to keep finding new ways to express oneself and the problems one is surrounded by. The simultaneous need and failure to do so, create a painful situation, in which the body plays a particularly crucial and rewarding role for its closeness to oneself and its general meaning for others. Thus is my incentive to explore those bodies "we fail."

1 Reading for Monsters

The protagonist of Djuna Barnes's novel *Nightwood* (1936), Robin Vote, comes across as a girl lost to the world, not subject to the usual bonds of love and desire, almost godlike. Barnes emphasizes her alterity in a variety of ways. Characterized in the parlance of the time as an "invert," Robin is described as a childlike being whose natural realm is a wilderness. She possesses animalistic features, and, like her eponym (the nightingale or robin), she is a nocturnal creature. As someone who goes out walking at night, her gender is obscured and made ambiguous; she roams the streets and, like her winged kin, attracts female partners. Robin is ultimately portrayed in the novel as an angel-like statue, seemingly ageless and, though withered, resistant to time and decay. She incarnates a fantasy: she is an ephemeral yet solid presence, and through this contradictory embodiment she can simultaneously fascinate and alarm those surrounding her.

Early-twentieth-century sexology classified the "invert" as a sexual deviant.[1] Inverts were said to exhibit confusion about their gender and were criminalized as outcasts or as cases for psychiatry. However, Robin is praised and admired by her friends and lovers. Though her gender and her queerness cause many of those around her to fear and be contemptuous of her, *Nightwood*'s protagonist nonetheless gleams like a beautiful painting.[2]

1　For more on the history of the invert, see Cohler 2010.

2　Queerness here stands not only for the character's sexual orientation, but also for the dislocation or the disturbance of representational traditions, linked to heteronormative ideals of gender and sexuality.

The "female invert" here becomes the exceptional love object, the deviant turned into a prince.

Barnes's novel not only exposes the historical and cultural construction of deviance, but, more importantly, brings the "monstrosity" of social, racial, and gendered difference close to the reader. Robin, said to be in danger of falling into a life that was "a monster with two heads" (65), avoids doing so only by constantly negotiating her otherness with her friends and lovers. Moreover, she wavers between distance and closeness, detachment and intimacy, to those around her as well as to the reader. In this way, the book links the heroine's construction of otherness to the reader's sense of self in a way that is partly alienating, partly pleasurable. As Matthew O'Connor, another character, reflects:

[W]hat is this love we have for the invert, boy or girl? It was they who were spoken of in every romance that we ever read. The girl lost, what is she but the Prince found? The Prince on the white horse that we have always been seeking. And the pretty lad who is a girl .... They go far back in our lost distance where what we never had stands waiting; it was inevitable that we should come upon them, for our miscalculated longing has created them. ... [They are] the living lie of our centuries. When a long lie comes up, sometimes it is a beauty; when it drops into dissolution, into drugs and drink, into disease and death, it has at once a singular and terrible attraction. (145-46)

In Matthew's words we find a fascinating synchrony between repulsion and attraction, desire and horror, romanticism and reality, truth and lie, love and hate, and masculinity and femininity. Those seeming contradictions are combined here, almost like the sensations one experiences when biting into a foul-smelling yet delicious-tasting fruit. I take them as a starting point to analyze the productivity of the simultaneously abhorrent and desirable characteristics of "gender deviance."

Matthew's monologue sheds light on gender inversion and same-sex desire in the interwar years, a period when eccentric otherness, even as it flourished and became the object of scientific research, was feared and persecuted. It indicates the novel's struggle with the limits of modern perceptions of "sexual inversion" in contrast to an idealized, romantic version of gender ambiguity and homoerotic love. In this sense, *Nightwood* bridges two historical phases: the nineteenth-century origins of sexology and the gay liberation movement of the 1960s and 70s. My discussion here seeks to trace the influence of both of these periods on contemporary normative gender and sexual identities.

The scientific study of human sexuality emerged at the end of the nineteenth century. Sexology was represented by psychologists and physicians who studied sexual behavior, most notably among them Richard von Krafft-Ebing, Sigmund Freud, and Magnus Hirschfeld, The British sexologist Havelock Ellis coined the term "sexual inversion" as a way to describe male homosexuality without taking part in the prevailing Victorian moralism toward sexuality (2007/1927). Ellis aimed to de-criminalize homosexuality by declaring it a congenital anomaly. Male homosexual behavior was not motivated by an abnormal psyche that was to be punished for its variance from the norm; rather, it was defined as a mere physical abnormality. Lesbian sexuality, however, was explained as "true inversion," ascribing masculine desire to women who were attracted to other women. Here, sexuality and gender identification became intertwined. Similarly, with the development of Freud's psychoanalytic studies and the synthesis of anatomical and psychological reasoning, the sexuality of fetishists, masochist, sadists, and other "perverts" came to be seen instead as forms of personal identity.[3]

The invert consequently embodied in one subject not only sexual diversion, but also gender variation. The concept of inversion, which began to reveal sex and gender as comprising culturally institutionalized and practiced conventions, challenged the seeming naturalness of "true" maleness or femaleness (cf. Freud 2000, Hirschfeld 1991, Krafft-Ebing 2011).[4] Representing neither one sex nor quite the other sex, the invert ultimately became a figure for the fearsome disruption of the order of things. Yet at the same time, the invert, up to the present (the abandonment of the term notwithstanding), symbolizes a poignant phenomenon of human corporeal existence: the undecidable and multiple nature of the conjunction between the self and the body. The link between bodily abnormality and non-normative behavior has been observed especially in relation to

---

3   For an overview of the history of sexology, see Bland and Doane 1998.

4   See Foucault 2003: 87. Foucault contends that since antiquity the monster, as a half-human, half-bestial creature, signified a violation of the laws of nature as well as a fundamental confusion of societal laws.

sexuality. However, other bodily markers – such as specific racial characteristics, and those signifying class, age, and non-normative physical attributes – have been stigmatized and added to a catalogue of monstrous corporeality.

In this sense, the invert and the monster share a history.[5] While the invert was born mainly out of scientific research, the creation and celebration of monsters has taken place within everyday discourse throughout history.[6] I want to focus on the coincidental, yet historically meaningful, overlap of monsters and inverts, of which *Nightwood* is a particular manifestation. In Barnes's novel, neither the invert nor the monster is explicitly brought to the reader's attention. Instead, what marks *Nightwood*'s characters as inverted and monstrous is woven into the structure of the plot and unfolds only in the intimate encounter between the fictional figure and the reader. The creation of monstrosity thus exemplifies what Judith Halberstam has termed the "technology of monsters."

In her analysis of Gothic literary fiction, she observes: "The monster's body is a machine that, in its Gothic mode, produces meaning and can represent any horrible trait that the reader feeds into the narrative" (1995: 21). The surrealist novel *Nightwood*, like its premodernist Victorian predecessors, offers itself as an "open book" to be filled with the reader's desire for horror and relishing of repulsion. Yet, in contrast to the way most Gothic novels convey the experience of horror through abnormal embodiment, *Nightwood* also invites the reader to relate to the obscurity of identity, the mutability of personality, and the multitude of human embodiments.

Out of the Gothic fiction of the nineteenth century came the literary monsters that have lodged themselves in the cultural imagination of the English-speaking world and beyond: Dr. Frankenstein's monster, Dracula, Mr. Hyde, and Dorian Gray. Despite the age-old history and cultural legacy of monsters in various Western traditions, these characters arguably mark, for the first time, human difference in a specific way. Because the body

---

5   In this book, I use the term "monster" to signify a narrative and visual tool to disturb common distinctions and apparent borders between the self and the other, between the human and the animalistic, between the "-abled" and the disabled.

6   For more on the promise of monsters, see Haraway 2004: 63-124.

was seen as enveloping a soul – which, as Foucault wrote in *Discipline and Punish* (1979) "[was] the prison of the body" (29-30) – the monstrous showed itself on the surface of the repressed body, a body in thrall to a monstrous soul. The figure of the monster was found simultaneously within and upon the body.[7]

Authors of Gothic fiction combined a variety of human differences to create a versatile version of the deviant body: as Halberstam states, their monsters were made of "lumpen bodies, bodies pieced together out of the fabric of race, class, gender, and sexuality" (1995: 3). The figure of Dr. Jekyll/Mr. Hyde is perhaps exemplary here. Dr. Jekyll produces within his own person, inside his own body, a perverse version of his respectable bourgeois body. As Halberstam observes:

Small, dark, and ugly, Hyde manifests the evil side of Jekyll in a physical form that marks vice upon the body and makes an essential connection between sin and hideous aspect. The body, in this novel, represents the aesthetic space in which sexuality and race conspire to determine human destinies. Hyde as a racial stereotype fixes sexual and racial difference within a body which combines horrific effect with Semitic and Negroid features. (ibid: 82)

The animalistic Mr. Hyde unites racial markers with deviant sexuality: his small, dwarfish, ape-like appearance hides within Jekyll's normal shape, thus showing his host to be a doubled body born from one being. The foreign body as abject body is constituted by bodies in bits and pieces, doubled or multiplied bodies, and bodies that combine seemingly conflicting human features. At the same time, the abject body retains a certain familiarity and confuses the boundaries between self and other.[8]

---

7   Halberstam defines Gothic fiction in her analysis as "the rhetorical style and narrative structure designed to produce fear and desire within the reader. ... Gothic infiltrates the Victorian novel as a symptomatic moment in which boundaries between good and evil, health and perversity, crime and punishment, truth and deception, inside and outside dissolve and threaten the integrity of the narrative itself" (1995: 2). I will follow Halberstam's definition of the Gothic in this chapter.

8   I am basing my argument on Kristeva's interpretation of the abject: "[The abject] is something rejected from which one does not part, from which one

At the beginning of the twentieth century, sexology and psychoanalysis connected the figure of the monster to so-called abnormal sexualities and gender identifications, like those we see in *Nightwood*. Much later, in the mid-to-late twentieth century, "queerness" emerged within social, political, and theoretical discourses to account in a non-derogatory way for persons who deviate from gender and sexual norms.[9] Those who were once "inverts" are today's "queers." Those who were once monsters are now the ugly, obese, disabled, black, old, or simply *unacceptable* bodies of today. Hence, normative discourses about the body are still influenced by the notion of the monster, but they have become more difficult to grasp. Their borders have become more fluid, their shades more varied. What we see in *Nightwood*, I argue, is a crossroads where these periods intersect.

Many of the descriptions of Robin refer to Gothic monster narratives as well as depict (almost contemporary) queer lives. This convergence allows me to engage in an analysis of ambiguous corporeality in a trans-historical way. Vague, ephemeral, and intriguing, Robin's monstrosity seems to have paved the way for a queer embodiment that productively plays with or appropriates the figure of the monster. As such, Robin stands for a form of deviance or queerness that marks the flesh of Western cultural discourse and runs like veins through the construction of the human body – as much today as it did a hundred years ago. On the basis of this telling history of corporeal ambiguity, I elaborate the notion of queer monstrosity, which reveals that binary gender and sex classifications cannot satisfactorily account for human bodies and the diversity of corporeal experiences. I focus on the "inappropriate" sexual behavior and disturbing identities of *Nightwood*'s characters.[10]

---

does not protect oneself as from an object. Imaginary uncanniness and real threat, it beckons to us and ends up engulfing us" (Kristeva 1982: 4).

9   While the term "queer" has and may still be used as a slur, it has also been reclaimed by gays and lesbians and transformed into a marker of positive identification (Butler 1997).

10 See Judith Halberstam on the notion of monstrosity as "queer category that defines the [normal] subject as at least partially monstrous" (1995: 27). Donna Haraway discusses the monster as inappropriate/d other, which means it is not to be fit into any categorization, and primarily "not to be originally fixed by difference" (2004: 69).

In the first part of this present chapter, I will draw on Judith Halberstam's analysis of the Gothic fictional monster (1995), in which she develops a theory of the technology of monstrosity. I will discuss *Nightwood* in relation to Mary Shelley's *Frankenstein* (1831) both to show Robin's "monstrous" traits and to differentiate her from her historical predecessors. Subsequently, with the help of Judith Butler's theory of performativity (1990; 1997) and Garrett Stewart's account of phonemic reading (1990), I will analyze the complicit relationship between *Nightwood*'s characters and the reader. Both of these concepts theorize language as an active agent in the construction of meaning and a person's subjectivity. Phonemic reading reflects on what is written between the lines, or on signification that occurs beyond the lexical meaning of words. The theory of performativity assumes that the social use of language, or the acting out of speech, has an effect not only on the meaning of words, but also on the subjectivity of the speaker, listener, or reader. *Nightwood*'s ambiguous plot urges the reader to get involved in making sense of the characters. I contend that the reader, just to make sense of the novel, must participate in the book's production of meaning.

Interested as I am in the role of affect in the construction of monstrosity, I will then reflect on *Nightwood*'s affective consequences for the reader and the reader's complicity in the cultural discourse of monstrosity. Although she refuses to adopt any normative identity, Robin is nonetheless desirable as a person. She is dependent on the reader, even as she manipulates and involves the reader affectively in her own creation. Through the reader's complicity, the figure of monster is here patently human-made, and cannot be diametrically opposed to the reader's or the theorist's subjectivity. Finally, I claim that monstrosity can serve as a queer category wherein the non-normative subject is a human being who eludes taxonomy, transgresses the boundaries between self and other, and challenges fixed categorizations of identity.[11]

---

11 Margrit Shildrick pointedly describes the monster in relation to the conceptions of self versus other in her discussion of Jacques Derrida and Donna Haraway: "the monster is not simply a signifier of otherness, but an altogether more complex figure that calls to mind not so much the other *per se*, as the trace of the other in the self" (Shildrick 2002: 129).

Gothic Monsters

In her book *Skin Shows: Gothic Horror and the Technology of Monstrosity* (1995), Judith Halberstam catalogues the traits of nineteenth-century literary monsters, comparing them to their successors in postmodern horror films. The earlier forms strongly inform these later efforts, but with telling differences, which show the transformed role of bodies in the construction of monstrosity. Halberstam posits the Gothic monster as a metaphor for the uncertain borders around the physical body. The stability of binary oppositions such as outside/inside, female/male, body/mind, and self/other dominated the older conception of monstrosity. In Gothic novels, what is hidden, unspoken, or silent is distrusted, even as they exert an inescapable fascination.

Contemporary representations of monsters, in contrast, are notorious for their obsession with visuality, or what Halberstam terms the "obscenity of immediate visibility" (1995: 1). The Victorian fascination with human bodies' unknowable borders and edges has morphed into a tendency toward excessive visibility. With the development of new technologies – especially the emergence of photography, film, and now the Internet – norms that attempt to govern the human body have changed. Through the extension of networks across social classes and national borders, the battle over the boundaries between the body's interior and its skin have turned into a struggle pitting the human against the "non-human." Through increasing virtuality and the individual's greater physical distance from manifestations of monstrous bodies (because of the emphasis on the visual), as well as through the influence of psychoanalysis, the horror of monstrous bodies was made psychological as well as physical. The twentieth-century monster became "a conspiracy of bodies" (ibid: 27). The human body has begun to serve as a new monster machine. Nonetheless, as Halberstam argues, what Gothic and contemporary forms of monstrosity share are the disruption of categories, the destabilization of borders, and the contamination of purity. What is monstrous about all of them is often, as Margrit Shildrick (2002) observes, their embodiment: "They are ... what Donna Haraway calls 'inappropriate/d others' (2004: 70) in that they challenge and resist normative human being ... by their aberrant corporeality." (9) Monsters are deformed, ugly, animalistic, overly sexual, and have large and powerful bodies. They are defined by their physicality, not their subjectivity.

Halberstam's reading of Mary Shelley's *Frankenstein* reveals possible analogies with *Nightwood*. One characteristic that Halberstam brings to the fore in her discussion of *Frankenstein* is an essential feature of Barnes's novel: the reader's investment in the construction of the fictional characters. Halberstam argues that the very nature of the monster transforms the reader of monster stories into a writer: "The monster, in its otherworldly form, its supernatural shape, wears the traces of its own construction" (1993: 349). Monstrosity unsettles boundaries between linguistic categorizations (such as those separating human and beast, woman and man, or reader and author), questions differentiations between self and other, and consequently affects a reader's interpretation of a text. The notion of mutual contamination between reader and character is a dominant theme in recent analyses of the Western monster discourse (cf. Halberstam 1995: 53-85 and Shildrick 2002: 68 86). When reading *Frankenstein*, Halberstam asks: "Do I read or am I written? Am I monster or monster maker? Am I monster hunter or the hunted? Am I human or other?" (1995: 36).

Dr. Frankenstein's creation can be a human or a monster, and can change from one to the other or display both aspects at the same time. By reading Gothic monster narratives as *technologies of monstrosity*, Halberstam claims a productivity that does not merely position the novel in a distanced discourse that others the sexually deviant, the racially undesirable, and the gender-unspecific person, but that allows for numerous interpretations, precisely because the monster transforms the fragments of otherness into one body (Halberstam 1995: 88-91). That body is not female, not Jewish, not homosexual, but it bears the marks of constructions of femininity, race, and sexuality (Halberstam 1993: 337). Halberstam writes:

Monsters ... can represent gender, race, nationality, class, and sexuality in one body. And even within these divisions of identity, the monster can still be broken down. Dracula, for example, can be read as aristocrat, a symbol of the masses; he is predator and yet feminine, he is consumer and producer, he is parasite and host, he is homosexual and heterosexual, he is even a lesbian. Monsters and the Gothic fiction that creates them are therefore technologies, narrative technologies that produce the perfect figure for negative identity. Monsters have to be everything the human is not. (1995: 21-22)

Consequently, the monstrous body calls attention to the plasticity or the constructed nature of its creation, calling into question the social practices used to classify deviance. Those practices are exposed as inventions of normative cultural powers.

Victor Frankenstein's scientific experiment, which leads to the creation of a horrendous monster, shows that to set truth in opposition to fantasy or imagination is to posit an untenable distinction. The outcome of the experiment, which had been minutely planned and supposedly rested on infallible scientific knowledge about the human organism, shares more with the fearful imaginations of human wickedness than with the "normality" of the morally good person who should have been the model:

Beautiful! – Great God! His yellow skin scarcely covered the work of muscles and arteries beneath; his hair was of a lustrous black, and flowing; his teeth of a pearly whiteness; but these luxuriances only formed a more horrid contrast with his watery eyes, that seemed almost of the same colour as the dun white sockets in which they were set, his shrivelled complexion and straight black lips. (Shelley 1998: 57)

Frankenstein's monster blends characteristics of the beautiful human being he should have been and the visual coding of the monstrous. He is more than simply human, animal, or "other." In his mixture of classifications, Frankenstein's monster not only undoes the singular category of the monster as "other," but he also, as Halberstam writes, "throws into relief humanness, because he emphasizes the constructedness of all identity" (1995: 38).

Bearing in mind this blending of human and monstrous features, I want to refer back to Halberstam's observation that the reader of Gothic fiction actively creates the monster with her desire to validate the "human." [12] The reader remakes the monster as other and alien. In Gothic monster narratives, the monster never becomes fully visible. In the case of Dr. Jekyll and Mr. Hyde, the monster hides within the figure/body of the book's respected, "normal" character. Similarly, in *The Picture of Dorian Gray*, the monstrous version of Dorian is both hidden in the painting, which has been banished to the attic, and in his young and beautiful body, which embodies his evil soul but which outwardly appears as a normal

---

12 I will use feminine pronouns throughout to designate the reader.

human self. As a consequence, these novels merely allow the reader to imagine the horrific spectacle of the monster, so that monstrosity is limited to the reader's imagination. It is this necessary element of imaginative action on the reader's part that finally makes the reader the author of the monstrosity she encounters.

In a similar way, Robin, I suggest, draws her reader into an imaginative world. Her rejection of unambiguous social categorizations – as well as her blurred appearance that results from her shadowy existence – demands an active reading. This sort of authorial role in conceiving Robin's character extends to the book's other characters as well. Robin is portrayed as a vessel, filled with the desires of her friends and lovers. They fabricate Robin as a character; overdetermined, she comes to exhibit traits that turn monstrous in the reader's imagination.

Like her Gothic predecessors, Robin is staged as being distant toward the characters who seek her out, but coming dangerously close to what they desire. She is human, yet also beyond humanity. However, compared to other monsters, Robin is much less invasive, indeed is barely perceptible: she seems to be something of a blank screen when compared with the Gothic monsters' demonstrative self-assertion. Robin's ephemeral presence creates space for others' self-identification. In this sense, she is a clean slate that offers a surface for others to reinvent their own selves. But, like her literary siblings, she is constructed by the fictional settings and by the reader. Through the layers of the other characters' identification with Robin, she gradually grows into a body that evades clear signification. Her body becomes a patchwork of images, sounds, and smells evoking those of the natural world; meanwhile, she stops functioning as a social agent. She becomes part of nature, silent and invisible:

Sometimes she slept in the woods; the silence that she had caused by her coming was broken again by insect and bird flowing back over her intrusion, which was forgotten in her fixed stillness, obliterating her as a drop of water is made anonymous by the pond into which it has fallen. (Barnes 2001: 151)

Robin's "natural" anonymity makes her a being without a name, history, or place. It is this blending of a monstrous yet almost indiscernible "nature" that motivates my reading of *Nightwood*. The monster serves here as a trope for a figure of near-absence and anonymity. Consequently, the monster must be brought into existence by the reader.

READING THE MONSTER

When *Nightwood* was published in 1936, the book was criticized as being tangled and obscure. The time and place of the setting changes constantly. Moreover, the plot unfolds across the different characters' pasts and memories. Barnes seems to have created the book's characters out of clay and animated them with a life independent of their author: they are formed so as to produce their own muddled stories.

The narrative is mainly set in Paris during the interwar period, and unfolds through a series of monologues and dialogues between the characters.[13] Robin Vote, a young American expatriate in France, is the main character, but also the least visible. She is the story's spirit, its engine and cause. All the narratives recounted in *Nightwood* seem to exist merely to conjure up her personality. Her relationships with the other characters form the skeleton of the story. Robin marries Felix Volkbein, becomes pregnant, and gives birth to their child. She then leaves him and their son and becomes intimately involved with Nora Wood. Her continuing promiscuity leads her to Jenny Petherbridge, for whom she abandons Nora. At the end, Robin, alone, seems to find fulfillment only in nature. Nora and Felix are devastated by Robin's behavior and seek advice from Dr. Mathew O'Connor, an Irishman and a former gynecologist who appears to understand more about Robin than anyone else. O'Connor dominates the novel with long, drunken tirades of self-ascribed wisdom. He is a cross-dresser and functions as spiritual advisor for Nora, Felix, and Jenny. Their lives are woven together almost by chance. What brings them together are their various complicated and shifting relationships to Robin.

Robin is a paradoxical character. She occupies the center of everyone's attention, but does not perform her part according to societal rules. She hardly ever speaks, nor is she regularly spoken to. Rather, the other

---

13 *Nightwood* is essentially plotless, but, as I argue in this chapter, a kind of plot is created by the reader on the basis of the novel's few signposts: the characters, the cities of Paris and Vienna, and a forest in North America.

characters speak *of* her. Moreover, the reader does not get a clear picture of Robin, no matter how much she is represented through the views of her lovers and the doctor. Robin seeps out of the narratives built around her. The more the other characters in the novel talk about her, the more she vanishes from the scene.

Barnes's novel exposes its readers to a seduction common to monster narratives. Stories such as *Frankenstein* and *Nightwood* are seductive because they refuse to offer a clear image. Reading the monster is always linked to an act of imagination, an act of visualization. Robin seduces her reader by offering entry into an imaginary, fantastic world. Yet she herself eludes visualization because she can transform herself from one thing into another: at first a wife who is to lead a mother's life, then a woman in a lesbian relationship who denies ever having given birth to her son. She becomes a masculine woman, who wanders unpredictably the nightscape of Paris according to her desires. Later, we see her fused with the landscape, barely distinguishable from animals and plants.

Robin's tendency to slip from one particular body, gender, and sexual identity into their opposites – woman/boy, human/beast – likens her again to the monstrous figures of Gothic narratives. As Halberstam remarks:

The tendency within Gothic fiction of one thing to slip into its opposite ... makes mincemeat of any notion of binaries. This is one of the reasons that it becomes so difficult to pinpoint the political impetus of any given Gothic text but it also is what produces the multiple web of interpretations that mark Gothic as both highly readable and unreadable. (1995: 179)

Nightwood's unreadability similarly expresses itself through Robin's fleeting and always transforming nature. Paradoxically, the book's readability is enabled by the author's excessive recourse to visuality. The many references to paintings, landscapes, and other visual markers give the reader the illusion that she is seeing into Robin's world, and provides further impetus to continue this sort of looking.

In the following passage, Robin is depicted as a spectacular shape-shifter, taking on the forms of a painting, a wild animal, and an actor, moving between cultural and natural realms:

> Like a painting by the *douanier* Rousseau, she seemed to lie in a jungle trapped in a drawing room ... thrown in among carnivorous flowers as their ration; the set, the property of an unseen *dompteur*, half lord, half promoter, over which one expects to hear the strains of an orchestra of wood-wind render a serenade which will popularize the wilderness. (Barnes 2001: 31)

The *dompteur* is invisible: he tames flowers and animals from an unseen position. But he creates visibility: the domesticated wilderness is rendered visible by standardization and unification. Robin belongs to this kind of nature, and becomes visible in the form of a painting that holds her within the frame of civilization – which is to say, categorization.

But who, we might ask, is the *dompteur*? The reader and, to a lesser extent, the characters around Robin. The reader has the power to play with the untamed and the uncultivated. She is not only entitled to get involved in the story, but effectively is forced to do so to make sense of the unstructured content of the book. The reader's imagination acts as both tamer and monster-maker. In a similar fashion, Felix, Nora, Jenny, and Matthew all struggle to read Robin to form a coherent picture of her. Their desire for her ambiguity paradoxically coerces her into readable structures. She is forced into identities: heterosexual, or lesbian womanhood, or motherhood. Yet even as her ambiguity is seemingly conquered by the amorous claims of others, Robin persistently reclaims her unfixed form by fleeing from those who love her.

As if he were Robin's comrade-in-arms, Matthew reveals identity to be a fiction, an illusion developed when one represses otherness. He describes himself as a monstrous being, an ugly man; whereas he would prefer to be the vigorous young woman that he imagines he might have been in a previous incarnation:

> *Misericordia*, am I not the girl to know of what I speak? We go to our Houses by our nature – and our nature, no matter how it is, we all have to stand – as for me, so God has made me, my house is the pissing port ... In the old days I was possibly a girl in Marseilles thumping the dock with a sailor, and perhaps it's that memory that haunts me. The wise men say that the remembrance of things past is all that we have for a future, and am I to blame if I've turned up this time as I shouldn't have been, when it was a high soprano I wanted, and deep corn curls to my bum, with a womb

as big as the king's kettle, and a bosom as high as the bowsprit of a fishing schooner? And what do I get but a face on me like an old child's bottom. (ibid: 81)

In exposing how social norms are limited according to the construction of fixed identities, Matthew also addresses the reader and her reenactment of gender categorization. In engaging with the figure of Robin, we must be aware that the uncertainty she provokes is built into binarism. Her ambiguity refers back to the oppositions between man and woman, human and animal, homo- and heterosexual, citing each of them all at once. There is no third term. The reference to the "normal," which here shows its mocking side, might be experienced as the biggest threat posed by the monster: its disruption of meaning through its excess. Monsters cannot be contained, yet they continually produce new meanings, unsettling the ground of knowledge.

Here, though, I would differentiate Robin Vote from Gothic monsters. Monsters in Gothic narratives are produced as perfect figures for negative identities, as Halberstam points out: "[They] have to be everything the human is not and, in producing the negative of human, [Gothic] novels make way for the invention of human as white, male, middle class, and heterosexual" (1995: 22). Gothic monsters fashion meaning through categorization, serving as normality's antithesis. Robin, conversely, is not so much a figure of negative identity as a creator of *non-identities*.

When Margrit Shildrick connects the history of the monstrous with postmodern feminist deployments of embodiment, she observes that social criticism can be productive in this regard precisely because of an emphasis on the body's fluidity: "As long as we resist the impulse to recapture, as it were, those undecidable and fluid forms of embodiment that mark out the monstrous, then the encounter with the strange(r) will be the grounds for a radical rethinking of the concept of the selfsame" (2002: 132). Comparably, Robin's renunciation of identity opens up space for desires outside of those that can be fit into a system of binary oppositions. Not only does Robin challenge the "normal," but she also makes the reader invent new identities out of her own body and desires: Robin's deviant "otherness" yields a pleasurable acting-out of the perverse indeterminacy of queer or transgender identities. Her gender-monstrous body serves as a stage to perform spectacular events of love, desire, sadness, madness, bestiality, and outrageous sexuality.

Robin's nightly excursions into the gloomy underworld, her sexual attraction to men, women, animals, and other natural phenomena, her boyish physiognomy (even after having given birth): all make her a queer and gender-crossing person. Her loneliness, her wandering and not belonging, her evasion of visual categorization identify her as neither quite man nor quite woman, neither hetero- nor homosexual, neither human nor beast. This lack is what, precisely, attracts the characters surrounding Robin to her. They use her ambiguity to fulfill their own desires; they expect her to take on the identities they create for her. Felix wants her to be his wife and a mother to his son. Nora pictures Robin as the stable partner she needs to cope with her anxieties. Jenny projects her existence as social outcast onto Robin. To all of them she figures as an empty sign, filled by whatever they choose to see in her. Robin's very body shifts: her boy's anatomy is transformed to that of a pregnant woman's; Nora even compares Robin to her dog.

It is almost as if Robin is part of a Freudian *fort-da* game: by disappearing and reappearing, Robin stands in for the little child's object and, as Freud theorized, allows the child – in this case, her lovers – to manage the anxiety of the mother's absence. (Freud 1961: 9) The characters in *Nightwood* use Robin as their *fort-da* object to represent and control their need for an affective relationship. Interestingly, Robin does not in the least represent a motherly type; yet, much like the child's object, abstracted from human form, she symbolizes a presence or realness that is missing from the lives of Nora and her friends. Does Robin also stimulate in the reader a longing to fill the relational void of childhood and of possibly unsatisfactory identification? If so, the reader not only produces her monstrosity, but also makes an object out of her; thus, in one body, Robin is monster, human, beast, and object.

In "Atavistic Perversions and the Science of Desire" (2001), Dana Seitler observes how the connection between ambiguous genders and bestiality becomes productive in texts such as *Nightwood*: "These texts, positioning their main characters down on all fours, and thus producing equivalencies between animality and sexuality, point to a shared project of making social problems identifiable and resolvable in the body that extends beyond the limits of generic convention" (544).

This *sharing*, I would like to stress, implicates the reader who, with her own bodily experience, brings to life the monster as a living creature.

Prompting the construction of Robin as a monster, *Nightwood* recalls the meaning-production achieved by Gothic monsters via several narrative devices: the disruption of linearity in plot and structure; the confusion of the roles of author, reader, and character; and the reversal of monster and monster-maker (Halberstam 1995: 19-20).

Robin has no narrative voice, and she tends to be silent and evasive. She flees, she wanders, she strays: such would seem to be the extent of her actions. At the end of the novel, she almost loses human identity, turning into a creature that resembles a dog. For the reader, and for Nora, she becomes a *beast*: "And down she went, until her head swung against [the dog's]; on all fours now, dragging her knees. The veins stood out in her neck, under her ears, swelled in her arms, and wide and throbbing rose up on her fingers as she moved forward" (Barnes 2001: 152). Even before this radical transformation, her husband Felix, trying to imagine what kind of creature she might be, describes her as

gracious and yet fading, like an old statue in a garden, that symbolizes the weather through which it has endured, and is not so much the work of man as the work of wind and rain and the herd of seasons, and though formed in man's image is a figure of doom ... Thinking of her, visualizing her, was an extreme act of the will. (ibid: 37)

An extreme act of the will, it should be noted, that is also required of the reader. Here again, the merging in Robin of objecthood (statue), the elements of nature (rain, wind), and animality (dog) demands an act of sense-making that goes beyond our usual terms. It reminds us again of the various roles assumed by a reader of Gothic fiction to meet the challenges of the monster narrative. When Halberstam writes that "[t]he reading subject (but also the characters and seemingly the writer) of the Gothic is constructed out of a kind of paranoia about boundaries," (1995: 36) she ascribes to the reader an active, albeit involuntary, position. The reader, akin to the novel's characters, is confronted with her own paranoia about unstable meaning. Robin, the mirror image of this fear, does little to relieve it.

When Nora confronts Dr. O'Connor with her desperate wish to know more about Robin, he tells her that "Robin was outside the 'human type' – a wild thing caught in a woman's skin, monstrously alone, monstrously vain" (Barnes 2001: 131). Even though the doctor situates Robin in a woman's body, the reader is still left with the difficulty of pinning her down with a fixed identity. Caught in her own skin, Robin is a wild thing, or a woman who does not naturally have or own a woman's body. One can picture her as a naked creature squirming in an outer skin that fits neither her body nor her mind and soul: a grotesque, unpleasant, yet touching image.

Robin's defiance of self-identified subjecthood, which reciprocates others' desires, is what makes her monstrous. Like monsters, Robin is marked by being apart, by being viewed as a spectacular object, and by having a body that does not conform to corporeal norms.[14] At the end of the novel, Robin seems to find a home in the guise of a creature that is half-human, half-beast, and that figures as the sexualized Other:

Robin began going down. Sliding down she went; down, her hair swinging, her arms held out ... on all fours now, dragging her knees. ... Then she began to bark also, crawling after [the dog] – barking in a fit of laughter, obscene and touching. The dog began to cry, running with her, head-on with her head, as if to circumvent her; soft and slow his feet went. He ran this way and that, low down in his throat crying, and she grinning and crying with him; crying in shorter and shorter spaces, moving head to head, until she gave up, lying out, her hands beside her, her face turned and weeping; and the dog too gave up then, and lay down, his eyes bloodshot, his head flat along her knees. (ibid: 152-53)

Robin and the dog seem to melt into each other, becoming barely distinguishable. Although in their rawness and vulnerability they are like children, Barnes's description of the two bodies is sexually tinged. She thus positions the reader morally, vis-à-vis the reader's fears of having animalistic or pedophilic desires. This danger is commonly triggered by the monstrous, since, as Halberstam observes, the monster is experienced as a

---

14 According to Shildrick, the bodies of monsters "radically [disrupt] morphological expectations" and fail to "approximate to corporeal norms" (2002: 2).

poisonous infection, contaminating the good citizen's moral and spiritual purity with abnormal longings.[15]

Not only, then, is the reader *Nightwood*'s monster-maker, but she is made complicit with her fictional creation. As much as Robin comes into existence through the reader's and the other characters' acts of portraying her, it is she, after all, who causes them to take up their roles as actors. Consequently, reader and character share each other's conditions of becoming. This mutually dependant relationship is the basis for what I call, alluding to the work of Judith Butler, *performative reading*.

PERFORMATIVE READING

With the help of Butler's theory of the performativity of language (1997), I aim here to analyze how the reader creates Robin as monstrous and how, conversely, Robin makes the reader complicit in her own monstrous creation. In her account of the formation of subjectivity, Butler contends that, as linguistic beings, we are inevitably called into existence by socially sanctioned forms of address (1997). These forms of address put us in our place by naming us within the categories of gender, race, class, and culture. Those forms of address ("you are a girl," "you are black," "you are a stranger," etc.) designate us not only as persons but also as embodied beings. Butler stresses the somatic dimension of the linguistic process of becoming a subject. Indeed, on the site of the body our subjectivity is both sustained and threatened through modes of address. In this sense, the possibility or the foreclosure of social existence is enacted through our bodies. In this corporeal manifestation of language, the performative character of speech acts, as J. L. Austin has conceived of them, becomes evident.

In *How To Do Things With Words* (1955), Austin conceptualizes a theory of speech in which certain forms of speech do what they say rather than just say what they mean. Distinguishing between illocutionary and perlocutionary acts, he assigns to the former the aspect of acting by saying something, and to the latter the achievement of an ensuing act by saying

---

15 See Halberstam 1995 on *The Picture of Dorian Gray* and its reception after its publication in 1891.

something. The act of saying something (locution) often becomes, in these cases, a physical performance motivated by language. Although Austin's theory distinguishes in detail which forms of speech can successfully function as acts, I want here merely to point to the general capacity of language to perform or trigger corporeal action. The performative link between language and the body, which Butler analyzes in relation to gender performativity (1990), hate speech (1997), and the vulnerability of bodies (2006), is my focus here, because it allows me to account for the corporeal dimension of Robin's literary presence in *Nightwood*.

The "acting out" of speech results in physical effects. It hails our bodies into social existence, it prompts the cultural sense held by bodies, and it grants, or denies, social recognition to these bodies. In Butler's analysis of excitable speech, in which she employs Louis Althusser's concept of interpellation,[16] she writes:

Language sustains the body not by bringing it into being or feeding it in a literal way; rather, it is by being interpellated within the terms of language that a certain social existence of the body first becomes possible .... The address constitutes a being within the possible circuit of recognition and, accordingly, outside of it, in abjection. (1997: 5)

Putting words into practice, the body enacts and repeats the social conventions of its time and place. It acts as reader or interpreter of everyday speech situations.

Against this background, Butler explores how gender is constructed through particular corporeal acts and how, through the use of such acts, gender norms can be transformed. She ascribes to the body the ability to realize possibilities that exceed those of a binary gender system whose boundaries are set by cultural norms: "the gendered body acts its part in a

---

16 Butler uses and develops Louis Althusser's concept of interpellation, which describes how an individual is transformed into a subject by responding physically to a shout from a stranger in the street. "Hey you!" triggers a physical response in a human being; language here acts as social agent and accounts for a subject's social recognition. See Althusser 1971: 170-86. Butler theorizes furthermore the critical and potentially dangerous sides of social interpellation. See Butler 1997. See also chapter 1 of Silverman 1992.

culturally restricted corporeal space and enacts interpretations within the confines of already existing directives" (1988: 526). As Butler observes, all bodies are culturally constructed and are thus confined within certain norms; they cannot be read or even exist outside such norms, but they can performatively reenact and potentially transform the import of the directives. Notions of gender and other corporeal norms are thus constantly in the process of actualization through our bodies, which perform them, and without which they would be insubstantial.

Halberstam, similarly, observes a particular kind of performativity in Gothic monster narratives. In her account, Gothic novels possess a capacity for meaning-production that resides no less in the text or in the novel's form than in the reader's complicit reading, which is informed by the same norms that Butler reveals as constitutive of the body's restrictions and possibilities. Halberstam contends that "[the] monstrosity of *Frankenstein* is literally built into the textuality of the novel to the point where textual production itself is responsible for generating monsters" (1995: 31). *Frankenstein*, in its very structure – in which the sum of its parts exceeds the whole, and relations are skewed between author and reader and author and narrator, as well as among characters – is a monster text; its distorted textuality, in which portrayals of its characters exceed categorization, draws the reader into the hideous production of monstrosity.

In *Nightwood* I observe a form of textuality that corresponds to Halberstam's characterization of *Frankenstein* in that *Nightwood*'s structure contorts common role allocations among author, reader, narrator, and characters; yet Barnes's novel so abstracts textual form that it becomes *informe*, "a procedure to strip away categories and to undo the very terms of meaning/being," in Rosalind Krauss's definition of the term (Bois and Krauss 1997: 155).[17] The formless textuality of *Nightwood* strips the human being of her characteristics and makes her simultaneously *isotropic* (uniform in all directions) and variously identifiable. The defiance or negation of form in *Nightwood*, contrary to *Frankenstein's* excess, might pose a problem to Butler's and Halberstam's theories. As much as the novel's text engages the reader in a complicit and active role of sense-

---

17 For more on the Formless see Bois & Krauss 1997, Krauss 2000, and chapter 5 of the present book.

making, it also cancels out any clear form of identification with the book's main character.

The textual denial of form seems to infect Robin, to dissolve her form so that it seeps out of the book and creates uncharacteristic meaning. As such, the novel adds another model of readership to that of Halberstam. The monster-making reader is here augmented by the indistinct reader – a reader who is drawn into the formless that Krauss, alluding to Bataille, describes as follows:

[Categorical] blurring [is] initiated by the continual alteration of identity. It is not just some kind of haze or vagueness in the field of definition, but the impossibility of definition itself due to a strategy of slippage within the very logic of categories, a logic that works according to self-identity – male, say, or female – stabilized by the opposition between self and other: male versus female, hard versus soft, inside versus outside, life versus death, vertical versus horizontal. (Krauss 2000: 7)

The indistinct nature of textuality, plot, character, and reader in *Nightwood* reflects the impossibility of defining Robin as male or female, human or beast, young or old. This observation, and the blurred relation between reader and character as self and other, lead me not only to identify the reader's complicity in the monster-making process, but to further direct me to the question of how Robin can be pictured and related to – if, that is, such relations between Robin and the reader are even possible. With the help of Butler's theory of discursive performativity, and by a focus on her concept of gender performativity, I will try to answer this question.

SUBVERTING PERFORMANCE

As we saw, Butler shows that interpellation is a performative speech-act, through which a subject is first hailed into existence by linguistic conventions (such as "hey you!" or "it's a boy!"), and through which he or she can act as a social agent by citing or repeating the same linguistic practice (1997: 39). If, however, a subject is not recognized as human, and thus not hailed into a social community, she or he fails to participate in the discursive performativity (14) required to sustain a self. In these terms, Robin cannot be hailed into social existence.

When Butler describes gender performativity as the positing of an anticipation of a gendered "essence," she adds that this seeming essence is no more than the constant repetition of certain acts and gestures. Butler further argues that these acts, gestures, and enactments of desire "are *performative* in the sense that the essence or identity that they otherwise purport to express are *fabrications* manufactured and sustained through corporeal signs and other discursive means" (1990: 185). She thus concludes that gender is a "corporeal style" that suggests the construction of meaning.

In light of Robin's formlessness, we should ask: how does she perform her gender? It seems as if Robin altogether lacks corporeal style, which makes her a special case for Butler's theory. If human features, which manifest themselves also in attributes and acts, are missing or blurred, how can a subject become intelligible? Butler's analysis of drag performances as highly performative as well as potentially subversive might be applied to Robin in one way, yet not in another: drag performances destabilize the distinctions that constitute the reigning discourse about gender, the distinctions between the natural and the artificial, depth and surface, inside and outside, self and other.[18] While drag mostly expresses itself on a well-lit figurative or literal stage, and makes itself heard, seen, and felt in an excessively expressive way, Robin's (anti-)performance contains no eye-catching and forceful accessories. She does not dramatize, imitate, or parody gender roles as they are commonly understood.

In this sense, Robin does not seem to perform gender at all. As we saw, she can at most be seen as an imaginary or phantasmal manifestation of the other characters' gestures, bodily acts, and desires. She does not perform an actor's role; instead, her audience takes over. Unlike the drag performer's audience, which despite being invited to watch and engage in the spectacle is always beyond the stage, Robin's audience – that is, the people surrounding her – *embody* the stage they put her on. Robin's refusal or incapacity to perform deprives her of social recognition, yet it liberates her from what we might call the "imperative to perform."[19] Instead, the other characters and the reader must perform *her*, and must perform *for* her.

---

18 For more on drag performance, see Butler 1990 and 1997.

19 Jon McKenzie wrote an insightful book on the different meanings and consequences of performance and performativity in different cultural and

As an anonymous and unspoken life-form, Robin loses the privilege of being interpellated as a social being. In this sense, she suffers from what Butler describes as the loss of context, which also diminishes her chance at what Butler terms "linguistic survival" (1997: 4). Robin is exposed to the opinions and views of her companions. And although they do not mean to injure her, they cannot rescue her as she drifts away from language and social meaning. Butler's observation on the effects of injurious speech seem to apply to Robin's loss of place:

The speech situation is thus not a simple sort of context, one that might be defined easily by spatial and temporal boundaries. To be injured by speech is to suffer a loss of context, that is, not to know where you are. ... To be addressed injuriously is not only to be open to an unknown future, but not to know the time and place of injury, and to suffer the disorientation of one's situation as the effect of such speech. Exposed at the moment of such a shattering is precisely the volatility of one's "place" within the community of speakers; one can be "put in one's place" by such speech, but such place may be no place. (ibid: 4)

Although Robin seems not to know where she is or where she belongs, she also seems to be curiously beyond harm. Butler states that when subjects lose their context through exposure to linguistic or physical violence, their corporeal place in the world is threatened. Robin, however, is not in acute danger of physical injury. Yet, like the victims of injurious speech, she *is* in danger of never finding a place or role for her body to sustain a self. Robin lacks the conditions for a context as well as a self. Both absences are brought about by her failure to perform, which includes the failures to inhabit a singular body, to slip into a social role, and to articulate appropriate desire.

---

academic fields. One of his claims is that twentieth-century developments in research, technology, and management created an imperative to perform, which is reflected in the "efficacy of cultural performance" as much as in the "efficiency of organizational performance" and the "effectiveness of technological performance." Robin's non-performance, surveyed against this background, seems almost liberating: she leads a life beyond the aim or desire for effect, yet she exerts considerable effects on other people's lives.

Robin's inability, or denial, to perform a readable self challenges social and linguistic norms, which commonly enable yet also limit the possibilities of a subject's identity formation. My characterization of Robin as embodying a form of queer monstrosity here allows us to acknowledge not only the risk involved in losing recognition of the monstrous subject; but it also reveals the true "monstrosity" of the governing laws of social recognition, which are based on culturally constructed and naturalized bodily categories of gender, race, class, and humanness. The disturbance that Robin evokes in her reader exposes the technology of monstrosity as a potentially intimate, pleasurable, and affective process of engaging with the other, the ambiguous, and the un-categorized, a process that might allow us to account for the diversity of human forms of embodiment beyond the "monstrous." Reading for monsters in *Nightwood* results in a disruption of the discourse of monsters. The failure to identify the monster as monster reveals the monster's making.

2 Vulnerability

In an essay about perception and disability, W. J. T. Mitchell writes: "To be seen by the Other is to be disabled – engulfed by a wound in our world that drains all objects and spatial relations away from us" (2001: 394-95). Mitchell here expresses an important insight about the relationship between vision and the formation of the self. As soon as the other looks back at us, our vision becomes threatened because of our sense of insecurity, shame, and self-consciousness. The look of the other disables the projection of the self onto the other; instead, it exposes the self to the other. What does it mean to look at the other, who looks back at us, disabling us?

In a sequence in the documentary film *augen blicke N* (2005), by Gitta Gsell and Gesa Ziemer, a person of short stature descends the steps of an out-of-order escalator (Fig. 1). For Rika Esser, 85 centimeters tall, this is a technological monstrosity. She moves precariously downwards, holding onto the metal side-walls of the escalator, carefully taking one huge step after another. The fixed camera is positioned at the bottom of the stairs so that we witness her slow descent. Her progression reminds us of our own familiar awkward walk on the metallic and hollow-sounding steps, on which it's usually something of a struggle to keep our balance. The film inevitably recalls our experience of bodily hindrance in environments built to suit "normal" bodies for comfort and speed, which make up a great share of a busy world oriented toward efficiency and functionality.[1] Indeed, the

---

1   The escalator scene is also part of a video clip made by and used in a piece by the Belgian performance group "Peeping Tom Collective," *Le Jardin* (2001), choreographed by Gabriela Carrizo, Franck Chartier, and Simon Versnel.

passage in the film makes us realize that the practicality of everyday technologies might easily be directed against us, making us vulnerable.

Rika Esser's awkward approach, coupled with the tunnel-vision of the camera, implies a viewer's gaze in which her body is not only exposed to the vision of an other, but in which the viewer shares a visual narrative about physical vulnerability. As the viewer watches the short-statured and uncommon body approach, she not only empathically engages in the bodily experience, but also makes herself complicit in the construction of the viewing situation. Viewing the disabled other here involves the viewer in the vision itself.

Fig. 1: Screenshot from augen blicke N [Rika Esser]

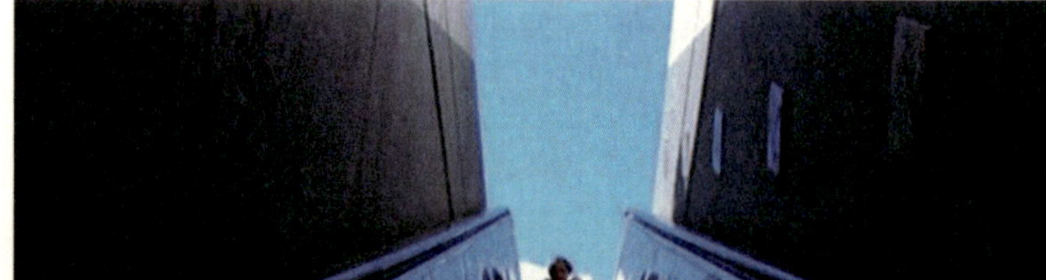

Source: Gitta Gsell (2005)

Conventionally, we project our look outwards, away from the body that sees, becoming blind to our own bodily predicaments. Yet when the sight of the disabled body triggers a shared corporeal experience in the viewer, as Esser's does in the torturous escalator scene, the viewer is thrown back onto the self: seen, or rather touched, or wounded by the other, as Mitchell observed. The blind spot of the seeing self toward its physical vulnerability is momentarily suspended; what is revealed is the subject's disablement vis-à-vis normative spaces and designs.

In her analysis of disability in contemporary performance practices, Petra Kuppers describes a similar phenomenon:

The presence of the disabled person is problematic in many social situations: it threatens a shift in the status quo, a momentary visibility of one's own body or self as potentially different, as one is faced by that which is 'disruptive.' (2003: 6)

However, the presence of Esser's body in the escalator scene adds something to this momentary visibility. The exposure of the disabled body within the artistic spheres of film or dance elicits not only the viewer's potential difference within a social context, but also her physical vulnerability to seeing and being seen by the other. Such an awareness of one's vulnerability might prompt a moment of thoughtfulness and reconsideration about the ways we commonly regard exceptional bodies.

In this chapter, I want to explore new ways of looking at disabled, imperfect, and extraordinary bodies by discussing *augen blicke N* (2005). The film provides insight into the bodily experiences of several dancers with physical disabilities, and suggests a certain productivity as well as an ethical necessity to engage in "vulnerably looking," as I would call it. In particular I would like to focus on one of the artists in *augen blicke N*, Raimund Hoghe, and his performance in the film.[2]

Both the film and Hoghe's choreography trace the vulnerable body in its potential to challenge the looks commonly projected onto corporeal difference. When Hoghe, in his *Lecture Performance: Throwing the Body into the Fight* (2000-1), reveals his buckled, visually unwelcome body to the audience, he exposes his vulnerable self as something shared and shaped by his spectators. The show elicits identification with a corporeal experience of vulnerability rather than with Hoghe's specific body or personality. Consequently, it informs the viewer of the risks involved in relating to another person physically and sensuously. I argue that to account for this mode of visual experience, and to explore practices that challenge a dichotomous conception of selfhood, we require an *aesthetic of vulnerability*.

For my argument, I primarily draw on the notion of "double exposures." In *Double Exposures: The Subject of Cultural Analysis* (1996), Mieke Bal shows how the photographic technique of double exposure is

---

2   *Lecture Performance: Throwing the Body into the Fight* (2000, first version), Académie Expérimentale des Théâtres, Paris. Text, Direction, Choreography, and Dance by Raimund Hoghe. Artistic Collaboration: Luca Giacomo Schulte.

used to make a composite image, created when the film is exposed to different light sources at independent points in time. Such images consist of two visual realities overlapping in the same picture. The viewer of the image discovers a new aspect of the world through the image's visual distortion.

What constitutes a viewer's vision of the world, in addition to the content or form of the image that she is looking at, is the gaze. In *Four Fundamental Concepts* (1978) Jacques Lacan differentiates the gaze from a subject's look by metaphorizing it as a camera-like "apparatus" whose function it is to locate the viewer "within the spectacle" (Silverman 1996: 131). The gaze socializes a viewer's vision and represents the presence of others in this vision.[3] In his analysis of the gaze as it pertains to the realm of painting and visuality, Norman Bryson writes:

Vision is socialized, and thereafter deviation from this social construction of visual reality can be measured and named, variously, as hallucination, misrecognition, or "visual disturbance." (1988: 91)

This socialized vision exposes a picture in yet another way: it opens up a relationship encompassing picture, viewer, and vision, which not only can lead to visual disturbances, but also might make us aware of the structural instability and vulnerability of the visual field.

In addition to Bal's theory of double exposure and Mitchell's account of seeing disability, I employ Judith Butler's notion of relational vulnerability. Finally, assisted by Margrit Shildrick's conceptions of monstrosity and an "ethics of risk," I seek to point toward the necessity of engaging visuality in a critique of physical reality. An awareness of shared physical vulnerability opens up space for the differentiation of vision. The act of looking becomes equally dependent on the viewer and the seen; it

---

3   Silverman (1996) extends Lacan's distinction of the gaze and the subject's look by giving agency to the "collective look." Lacan confers visual authority not to the look, but to the gaze. The cultural gaze determines how we are perceived as individual subjects. Silverman conceptualizes the gaze as that field of vision in which we can collectively try to transform the cultural screen through which subjects are perceived (19). She sees in this use of the "collective look" the possibility of "productive vision" (227).

becomes an exchange based on negotiated codes of humanness rather than a rigid opposition setting normality against deviance.

augen blicke N (entitled in English *Point of View*) investigates how the representation of disability performed on stage challenges how disabled bodies are commonly looked at in public. The German title *augen blicke N* is a play on words and encompasses the German words for "eyes," "instants," or "winks" (of the eye), as well as the verb "to look." The German title, more so than the English one, can be read as implicating the momentary, temporal, and unstable character of the act of looking, which is part of what the film seeks to expose through its conception of an aesthetic of vulnerability. The use of lower-case words in the title might be interpreted as emphasizing the *act* of looking (verb) rather than having the look be understood as an idea or concept (noun).

The artists in the film display their physical and cultural vulnerabilities as enabling: not only are they exposed to and afford a different worldview, but they also can show that looking at bodies is a precarious cultural practice, which reveals the vulnerability of every body. The visibility of disabled or uncommon bodies on the stage problematizes established views of persons with disabilities as other, tragic, helpless, or monstrous.

augen blicke N features five dancers and performance artists, each of whom explore the vulnerable body as an aesthetic figure on stage as well as in daily life. In interviews, which are interspersed with filmed sequences of their stage work, they discuss their everyday experiences and their intentions as choreographers. These interviews take place in dance studios, in a private living room, and in the public spaces of a museum and a café. The performances are shown unfolding on various theatrical stages. The viewer plays the roles of interviewer, listener, and spectator. As such, she becomes involved in a dialogic relation with the artists, who all respond to inaudible questions. Yet surely the viewer already knows these questions, since they have been posed so many times before, often unspoken yet manifested in everyday social situations by a curious, shameful, or shocked gaze: What is wrong with you? Do you need help? Doesn't anybody take care of you? What kind of creature are you? By responding verbally and visually to these mute and degrading questions, the artists in *augen blicke N* direct their looks back at the viewer. Hence, the spectator is exposed to the looks from and toward differently embodied persons.

The filmmakers call the attempt to create a look toward difference an "aesthetic of vulnerability" (*Ästhetik der Verletzbarkeit*). The ability to expose oneself as a vulnerable being (*das sich-verletzbar-zeigen-Können*) is conceptualized as the possibility of becoming-human or becoming-self for all bodies. This new aesthetic language should be provocative: it wants to scandalize the viewer, to show that what is outrageous is not the deviant body itself but our perception and interpretation of it. Gesa Ziemer, one of the filmmakers of *augen blicke N*, contends that the vulnerable body does not necessarily provoke vulnerability in someone else, but motivates a sensitive look that helps create a more inclusive, interdependent relationship with others.

Consequently, the vulnerable body can be seen not only as a corporeal figure exposed to social violence, but also as a reflexive figure that throws light on our own vulnerability – the vulnerability that is shared by every body. In this respect, the performers in *augen blicke N* establish the basis for a mutual recognition of vulnerability on their terms: namely, under the condition of a multiplicity of embodied difference. By interrogating these practices, they provide the ground for further reflections on the aesthetics of vulnerability.

DISTORTED VISION

In his essay, Mitchell calls for new visual practices in relation to disabled and extraordinary bodies. He argues that observing "disability" poses a problem for the way we commonly look at other people. Hence, we should question the applicability of critical visual models developed by feminist or queer theory in relation to people with disabilities. To account for the difference of disabled bodily experience, what is needed is a *seeing with*: a practical envisioning of how people with disabilities see the world. But how do we develop this mode of seeing, when seeing itself is typically defined as an outward projection from the seer onto the seen, from the self onto the other, the neutral onto the conspicuous? And when the position of the object is associated with passivity, inferiority, and powerlessness, while the spectator is bestowed with the power to see "how things are"?[4] Mitchell

---

4   See Bal 1996: 2. Bal describes the ambiguities involved in acts of exposure, in which the exposed object is made visually available, while the person who

suggests acknowledging that some things, such as the physical peculiarity of an unusual body, are more visible than others. However, this does not mean that the things that are usually unseen, like the specific worldview of a differently embodied person, are not there. If this is taken into account, we can see that "normal" vision is itself impaired, because it remains blind to "how things are otherwise."

In *augen blicke N*, Ju Gosling, webmaster and multimedia storyteller, shows how a spinal brace, fitted closely to her distorted back, limits her movements. And yet this constriction is experienced as freeing. Because the corset-like plaster cast prevents her from making certain movements, it allows her, paradoxically, to do more with her body. Gosling found it more liberating to move within certain boundaries – determined by her own body – than to move unrestrained. In her film/dance performance *Fight*, Gosling's brace is adorned with several small round mirrors, which reflect her able-bodied partner's face as the two bodies move closely together, touching and supporting each other.[5] The performance highlights the mutual dependency of the two bodies; it also shows that certain things about the viewer's body and her ways of seeing other bodies can be seen only through and with the body of the other, that of the disabled person. Gosling's performative exposure of her body on stage exemplifies the practice that, according to Mitchell, makes disability studies so important: it reveals "vision itself as necessarily built on seeing disability" (Mitchell 2001: 395).

Similarly, Petra Kuppers claims that disabled performers have the ability to expand the range of images customarily assigned to their bodies. Physically impaired performers are involved in the negotiation of two areas of cultural meaning: "invisibility as active member in the public sphere, and hypervisibility and instant categorization as passive consumer and victim in much of the popular imagination" (Kuppers 2003: 49). Because of its

---

points at the object gains epistemic authority over the exhibit by saying: "Look! That's how it is." This discursive gesture of exposing connects the authority of the person who "knows" (epistemic) with the presence of the object (ontological), and points to the discrepancy between the object's unidentified existence and what the viewer "knows."

5   Performed by Ju Gosling with Layla Smith. Costumes by Andrew Logan. The City Gallery, Leicester (2001).

special position within the cultural sphere, the disabled body can teach us about bodily representation, forms of visual mediation, and our abiding blind spots. Disability's hypervisibility, always linked to its dialectical counterpart, invisibility (Mitchell 2001: 393), highlights only specific markers of otherness and difference, whereas what is usually left unseen are those parts of a person that make her a sensual human being. Since this sort of hypervisibility, coupled with invisibility, is also crucial for the experience of disability, Mitchell suggests, it should lead us to dissect visibility and question the governing negative visual stereotypes of the other's body as freak or monster.

Mitchell's call for new ways of looking at others and his critique of the "-abled" who "stumble into the world of disability as though they were, in fact, blind" (ibid: 394), brings me to the task of considering a new aesthetic. If we agree with what Mitchell, drawing on Sartre, declares – namely, that "the act of seeing as such is … always under the threat of blindness or … constituted on the constant experience of blindness, failures of seeing, ignorance, overlookings, blinkings" (ibid: 394) – it is time to adopt aesthetic practices that teach us how to sense the risks of vision, and become knowledgeable about them.[6]

Norman Bryson's distinction between two ways of looking, represented by the gaze and the glance, points to different modes of involvement of the subject in the coproduction of the image. Bryson develops a notion of the gaze through and beyond the different conceptions of the gaze theorized by Sartre and Lacan. He describes how Sartre's watcher is objectified by the other's gaze, as well as vice versa (Bryson 1988: 96). Vision thereby remains within the fundamental opposition between object and subject, while admitting a relationality, probably unsymmetrical, between the seer

---

6   The call for a new look regarding disabled bodies has been formulated not only by Mitchell, but also by other disability scholars, such as Lennard Davis and Marquard Smith in Davis 1999 and Davis and Smith 2006. Others have also developed models of theory that call for a multiply sensual reengagement of the body through disabled corporeal experience: see Snyder and Mitchell 2001. What makes me specifically consider W. J. T. Mitchell's approach, however, is his radical critique of the assumption of the functionality of vision itself. He contends that through disability we can learn about vision as well as about our relation to the other.

loved one, he keeps moving toward the back of the stage, revealing his "real" hunched back, draped in the silk blouse.

The lights dim, and Hoghe is plunged into darkness. Then he illuminates his plaster suit with a lighter, allowing the flame's flickering glow to caress its shape. Through the keyhole effect caused by the lighter flame and the limited vision that it allows, the audience can now see only the displaced hunch at the front of Hoghe's body. It looks like bare skin, a nude bosom, a fragment of the body exposed to the look of the audience, vulnerable. But its desirability and beauty do not lie in its form. They come to reside in the look upon the exposed, yet respected, body of the other. In this scene, Hoghe makes a powerful statement about his own view of his body: by exposing his "deformity" on stage, it is transformed from a public spectacle into something intimate and private. He opens up a space for the audience to engage with his disabled body through a new and different relationship.

The human body, particularly the face, figures as the visual marker of humanness, a humanness that is under constant threat: of illness, deformation, and death, and of being appropriated by trauma, social misrecognition, and violence. To ascertain one another's humanity, individuals need to identify *as* and *with* what counts as human (Bal 2005: 154). This identification amounts to a form of communication between represented and representative members of a given community. If the double sense of identification – *as* and *with* – is structurally comparable to the ambiguity of representation – *of* and *as* – then certain types of bodies can lead to a crisis of identification based on appearance. Or, if certain bodies do not "appear" to be human, because of exclusionary and stereotypical cultural conventions of how humanness is representable and identifiable, these bodies call into question any stringent equation between what *is* human and how it is embodied or what it *looks like*. The looking subject's humanness becomes a site of risk. Such risk might eventually initiate what Bal calls "embodied reflection," leading to an awareness of the physical and cultural vulnerability we have in common (2005: 153-54).

In her critique of theoretical models that understand vision to be dominated by the viewer's absolute power over the object of the look, Bal insists that visuality should be analyzed on the basis of an (inter)active relation between subject and object, viewer and artwork (1996: 261-62). This suggests a parallel with speech: it assumes the act of looking to be communicative. To understand what one sees, one must recognize it as something that belongs to a visual system, which is shared and communicated among others. But what happens with the visual stimuli that we do not understand? Many of these, I suggest, unsettle the viewer, since they cannot easily be attributed to some other, foreign language: it is not commonly believed that there exists more than one visual sign system. Instead, un- or misrecognized images are banished to the world of the other, the deformed, the disabled, the unnatural, or the objectified.

On the basis of Bal's concept of embodied reflection, I suggest there is a need for what she describes as a "differentiation of vision that allows a differentiation of vision's relation to power" (1996: 262). This conception grants disruptive and marginalized images of this world a return to the visual domain of the human. To flesh out this approach, I will first look at Judith Butler's account of the risk of looking. Butler theorizes the ontological necessity and dangers of our physical relation to one another, and postulates the acknowledgment of a vulnerability that is socially and politically shared. In addition, Margrit Shildrick calls for what she describes as an "ethics of vulnerability."

RELATIONAL VULNERABILITY

Two of Butler's books are specifically concerned with vulnerability. In *Excitable Speech: A Politics of the Performative* (1997), in which she engages with the debate about the violent effects of language, Butler cautions that we should not underestimate the vulnerability of language to transformation and appropriation. *Precarious Life: The Powers of Mourning and Violence* (2006) is a response to the current global situation of heightened cultural and physical vulnerability, which has resulted in assaults upon the fundamental interdependency of the human/self on the alien/other. Vulnerability is again doubly conceptualized as an aspect of humanness, at risk of exposure and violence, as well as a productive agent in the relational constitution of the self.

In *Excitable Speech*, Butler posits the vulnerability of language to failure through paralysis and misrecognition, as well as through resignification and reinterpretation. One of Butler's examples is the history of the term "queer" in the United States and Canada. While it has and may still be used as a slur, it has also been reclaimed by gays and lesbians and transformed into a marker of positive identification. What had been an exclusively offensive term has now come to signify a positive subjectivity, subverting the hegemonic order of normal self versus abject other. This case illustrates the susceptibility of language to specific temporal and cultural conditions. It also reveals language's potential to wound and to denigrate a subject socially. But precisely because language is unstable and unpredictable, the acts of addressing and being addressed by others expose every subject to the vulnerability of life in the midst of others.

In *Precarious Life*, Butler assesses the poverty of contemporary conditions of representation. Through cultural discourses that other and de-humanize foreigners, criminals, purported sexual deviants, the politically persecuted, and those whose bodies are ambiguous, mainstream media representations offer reductive black-and-white oppositions. In this context, the image of a human face can be read as vulnerable only when it represents an abstract, captured, unlived form of the human. For example, the photograph of a black African child printed on glossy paper or shown in a television commercial usually triggers the effects the image-makers aim for: it provokes empathy or pity with a child, who, under the same regime of representational politics, is, as an adult, unlikely to be treated as a human being. The image pleads for the viewer's sense of humanity, but in fact represents the barbarity of contemporary politics. In Butler's eyes, the chief flaw of contemporary representation is its strict disqualification of or blindness to the precariousness of life as part of the human condition. Indeed, the only face to be readily recognized as human under such representational politics is utterly inhuman: fixed in eternity without traces of life, such as grief, loss, age, illness, or disability. It may even lack signs of experienced pleasure, ecstasy, or anger.

Butler argues that the current politics of representation are flawed in that they do not sufficiently acknowledge the fact that all lives are subjected to a "primary vulnerability to others" (2006: xiv). A shared human and corporeal vulnerability would highlight the dependency of subjects on the recognition of and by others as human. Butler makes a case for what she conceptualizes as a shared social vulnerability, which must be recognized to reveal how strongly all of us are socially and politically enmeshed in our perception of each other. This recognition, Butler continues, is fundamentally dependent on a set of norms that originates outside ourselves, outside individual subjects. For the norms through which a subject is able to recognize itself and others as human and therefore vulnerable beings are given via address.

Being addressed, called upon, is a necessary moment for coming into existence. Butler observes that to be addressed "constitutes a being within the possible circuit of recognition and, accordingly, outside of it, abjection. … One comes to 'exist' by virtue of this fundamental dependency on the address of the Other" (1997: 5). Precisely because of its double-edged nature, the structure of address is precarious, prone to failure and deprivation: "To be addressed is to be, from the start, deprived of will, and to have that deprivation exist as the basis of one's situation in discourse" (2006: 139). The recognition of the vulnerable aspect of the subject's being in relation to others is a necessary social endeavor, which becomes ethical when the frailty and the limits of the category of the human are brought to the surface.

Interrogating the instability of the human image vis-à-vis disability helps me to assess the ethical aspect of everyday representations of the normal body, supposedly opposed to the monstrous. Thematizing disability allows me to address three issues in relation to Butler's employment of vulnerability. First, the engagement with disability brings to the fore the limits of the category of the human. As we have seen in *augen blicke N*, the performers' humanity as people with disabilities is commonly unacknowledged. They figure as others who represent the polar opposite of certain culturally specific, bodily ideals, against which the human form necessarily – at least initially – defines itself. The human is characterized by its differentiation of itself from what it is not. This aspect shows a paradoxical feature of all dualistic categorizations. Human versus non-human, male versus female, disabled versus -abled – all demand that subjects belong unambiguously belong to one side or the other, even as they intrinsically foreclose the possibility of containing all subjects through their dual structure.

Second, disability highlights the body's particular capacity to evade representations of the human. Bodies cannot be fully seized by and transfixed in modes of representation: they grow, age, change appearance, get ill, and die. Bodies elude categorizations of the human even as they are the basis of the human form. Living bodies emblematically stand for life itself; their modification is a condition of becoming. Disabled bodies paradigmatically lack as well as exceed the means for categorization in that they make visible the body's transformational disposition. And third, disability addresses the socially enabling potential of corporeal vulnerability to express an as-yet-unidentified multiplicity of visions upon the world.

Butler introduces an important aspect of the dehumanizing effects of representation that might lead to a possible reappropriation of what can count as human: "For representation to convey the human," she writes, "representation must not only fail, but it must *show* its failure" (2006: 144). What is unrepresentable of the features of life, bodies, and persons must nonetheless aspire to be represented, even if such an attempt will fail to capture what it refers to: the human. For the human exists not solely in the representational image: it resides in the relational dependency between the image and its viewer, between the self and the other.

augen blicke N takes up in practical fashion this relationality of visual meaning around bodies. In their stage work, the artists show that the perception of other bodies is inherently linked to the act of perceiving with one's own body. Addressing the commonality of bodily experience, the performers provoke awareness that they perceive through their own embodied knowledge, past or present. Simon Versnel, for example, exposes his audience's complicity with the viewing situation when he, an overweight elderly man, pale and dispirited, sits stark naked on stage and recounts the sad and rather poignant details of his younger self's private life:

I had a house, a fantastic house. And I had a garden, a beautiful garden, full of flowers. I had a beautiful wife and a little girl. And I had a lot of friends. They're all dead now. And I had a little white doggy. Very cute, called Calypso.... Oh I had a lot of clothes, you know. Very chic. And a lot of underwear I had ... Sloggi? You buy four and you pay for three.[8]

Versnel's nakedness underlines that the security and happiness that were attained through common assets in the past were an illusion. They are all gone now, with nothing left but a vulnerable self, a body exposed to age and fragility.

---

8   Cited from the film and dance-theatre piece *Le Jardin* (2001), created and performed by Gabriela Carrizo, Franck Chartier, and Simon Versnel.

However, Versnel refers not so much to the transience of things and of life itself, but rather to the unsettling realization that his body is yet still there, clinging to him in a transmogrified state, transformed into a violable, unwanted accomplice inextricably linked to his present self. This realization emerges from his exposure to his audience, who are in turn exposed to their shameful gazes at Versnel's aged and helplessly nude body, as well as to their own nakedness as it has been experienced before others and themselves. The commonality of vulnerable embodiment becomes the condition for the emergence on stage of a humane image.

For Butler, conventional visual imagery fails to capture humanity because it does not represent the embodied precariousness of life, which is born from our relating to the other, from our being towards the world and our being addressed by the other. Images do not commonly convey their relationality to their viewer; they do not address the viewer's position vis-à-vis the image or depict her complicity in the production of meaning via images. Indeed, the political aim of visualizing the normative human as normal ultimately entails the depiction of a monster, with whom one cannot possibly identify.[9]

But what if, as Bal suggests, such images *also* address or look at their viewer, making an ethical demand upon her? Could not the objectified African girl with a hardly seen wink be hinting at her exposure under such unambiguous and inhuman conditions? What if these images fail to smooth over the discriminatory inconsistency, which divides the so-called human from its vital and constitutive counterpart, the monster? And which role does the body – in particular the disabled, the monstrous body – play in this spectacle of counter-exposing the human as standardized entity?

Again, I want to stress here the body's import in the relationality of the subject. Butler states that "[The] body implies mortality, vulnerability, agency: the skin and the flesh expose us to the gaze of others, but also to touch, and to violence, and bodies put us at risk of becoming the agency and instrument of all these as well" (2006: 26). The body exposes every

---

9   Butler refers to Emmanuel Levinas's notion of the *Other*, which is represented by the face of humanity (not necessarily a human face); the Other here is that which is intrinsically other to the self, but which, in facing the self, is also constitutive of the self's becoming. See Butler 2006: 128-51, and Shildrick on the monstrous other, 2002: 87-102.

person to a vulnerability that is inflicted or brought about by another, equally vulnerable being. This means not only that we are all vulnerable, but also that we are "physically vulnerable to one another" (2006: 27), meaning that we are all physically interdependent.

Butler imagines a relational community, in which we are all compelled to account for our interdependence, and so refrain from inflicting violence on each other lest we would violate ourselves. In this view, when we represent ourselves in society we are also bound to represent the ghosts of the world we are part of, the others, the deviants, monsters, and enemies whom we so desperately try to keep from impinging on our identities. Let me assume that this type of community is real, but that it is not brought to our awareness in everyday life. Hence, with the help of artistic productions such as *augen blicke N*, it might be possible to see how the exposure of physical relationality and vulnerability allows us to apprehend the dependency on others as something both productive and transgressive for the constitution of identities.

The question remains as to how vulnerability can be enabling. The most vigorous way to imagine the effects of vulnerability – through the power of physical violence – shows it unquestionably to be disabling, as Butler observes:

Violence is surely a touch of the worst order, a way a primary vulnerability to other humans is exposed in its most terrifying way, a way in which we are given over, without control, to the will of another, a way in which life itself can be expunged by the willful action of another. (2006: 28)

Not only is this violence most prominently directed towards the sufferer's body, it is also executed with the help of the violator's body. In line with Butler, I believe that we must attend to corporeal vulnerability and abide by our own exposure to recognize the vulnerability at the heart of our physical existence and being towards others. To formulate an "aesthetics of vulnerability," we must develop practices of encountering one another on a nonviolent basis; yet this is possible only if we accept that we all are potentially exposed to one another, and only if we distribute equally the rights to normalcy.

What makes the realm of vision productive for the critique of violence is the relation between visuality and corporeality that is inherent in the forms of aesthetic practices manifested in artistic works and in everyday life. As I have shown, visuality can produce violent effects, comparable to those of hate speech, as Butler observes (1997). At the same time, I also want to identify a promise to expose such effects and to counter them within the visual. Butler observes that excitable speech can turn into a counter-mobilization of injurious speech, adding that "[the] word that wounds becomes an instrument of resistance in the redeployment that destroys the prior territory of its operation" (1997: 163). Similarly, wounding looks can, in a different aesthetic context, be turned against their sender. Or, as Simon Versnel in *augen blicke N* shows on stage, harmful, depreciating vision can turn itself against its viewer by making her aware that, at some point in life, she may see herself as abject, other, and monstrous.

Consider again the scene in which Versnel presents himself naked on stage. In being exposed to the aging body, the viewer is confronted with normality's limits and hence to the failure of its customary visual standards. Versnel's audience is affected by his vulnerability to bodily change through age and illness: the growing belly, the increase of wrinkles, the loss of physical mobility and beauty, the reduction of the financial and social means required to live an attractive life. The viewer identifies not only with the shared vulnerability to the social and temporal exposure of the body, but also with a mutual humanness. To identify with a disabled, aged, or fragile person's physical experience makes the identification between self and other, as between human and human, an event of ethical value for the social recognition of people with disabilities. The body of Versnel becomes aligned with the commonality of physical experience. The scene dislocates the human from the scheme of visual, cultural, or gender difference, and positions it in the realm of mutual recognition, of potentially shared experiences of the body. Here, the representation of the human resides in the relation between the viewer and the seen. The relocation of the human opens up a new ontological horizon, characterized by our becoming vulnerable to one another.

ETHICAL VULNERABILITY

In drawing on Butler's two notions of vulnerability, I intend to develop a sense of vulnerability that brings into view two dimensions of bodily exposure: the social (linguistic vulnerability, the iterability of the subject) and the political (susceptibility to denigrating cultural representations and physical violence). Butler develops Jacques Derrida's notion of "iterability" as a productive form of the repetition of norms. In Butler's definition of performativity as a "reiterative" and "citational" practice (1993: 10, 109), she posits repetition as the basis on which conventions are built and without which we would not be able to understand what is being said or represented. Butler states that such repetition "enables a subject" (ibid: 95); by reciting practices that over time have become indications of femininity, for example, a subject can be recognized as a woman. Simultaneously, every repetition is inherently unstable and can at once exercise subversive as well as violent effects. If a subject is not recognized, because she fails to repeat conventional norms, she is punished for "doing" gender, race, or age inappropriately, or for behaving unnaturally. A subject is thus not only enabled by repetition, but is also vulnerable to its effects.

Butler's conception of vulnerability, however, lacks specificity. As much as the recognition of a general relational dependency and a mutual vulnerability is valuable for a reconfiguration of the opposition of the human versus the other, Butler's theory does not engage with the individual reality of visible differences. Some bodies more easily fulfill cultural expectations, while others, marked by corporeal undecidability or strangeness, are exposed to normativity more violently. To investigate the specificity of vulnerability in encounters with unusual, disabled, or allegedly monstrous bodies, I look at the way that Shildrick's notion of vulnerability complements Butler's. Doing so entails a reformulation of vulnerability, which takes me from the domain of the political and collective to that of the ethical and subjective. I accept this shift as being crucial for us to arrive at an aesthetic recognition of embodied difference at the level of subjective experience.

In *augen blicke N* Ju Gosling makes an argument for such a shift when she states how disabled persons, when in public, are detached from the personalities that inhabit their bodies:

The disabled body is always seen as a public body. It's always seen as a spectacle. People think they have the right to look at it, to categorize it and then to dismiss it and then to look away. ... In the same way they think they have the right to ask questions. Complete strangers can come up to you in the street and say: Well and what's wrong with you then?

Disability becomes public property in daily life as well as through representation. Disability is habitually disregarded as a viable form of life and embodiment, an integral part of personal identification and the development of a person's selfhood. In my analysis of the critical potential of the vulnerable body, it is thus important to situate unusual bodies, potentially *all* bodies – subjected to, yet also triggering, vulnerability – within the context of shared but subjective experience.

In her book *Embodying the Monster: Encounters with the Vulnerable Self*, Shildrick reconceptualizes the concepts of vulnerability and the monstrous. Analyzing corporeal difference within a posthumanist ethics, she allows these concepts to reflect on the relations of self and other, and touches on the fundamental and still culturally unacknowledged aspect of selfhood as formed in and through the concept of the other. The monster in her work stands for ambiguous embodiment in various forms: conjoined twins, cyborgs, hybrids, and racially othered or disabled bodies.

For Shildrick, the body that defies categorization and thus occupies many facets of the normal offers the promise of shattering the belief in a self-sufficient subject. Shildrick suggests "new ways of conceptualizing disability that demand a deconstruction of existing ethical parameters in the light of an always already vulnerability as the condition not only of all bodies, but of all embodied selves" (2000: 217).[10] She aims to reconfigure

---

10 In another passage, Shildrick also highlights the important fact that healthy bodies are not viewed as uniformly invulnerable, whereby especially infants and children, as well as women and older people, are commonly seen as being more dependent than others. This observation on the one hand stresses the compromise of idealistic corporeal schemas like normality, inviolability, stability. On the other hand, it speaks of the *paternalizing* tendencies of a society based on hierarchical structures that distinguishes only a certain class of bodies, on which the privilege of a fully autonomous, self-governed life is bestowed.

vulnerability as an "inalienable condition of becoming" (ibid: 226). To participate in an ethical encounter with the others who surround us, this condition must be recognized as an enabling quality rather than one that signals physical dependency, weakness, and victimization.

Within feminist conceptions of ethical relationality, the model of "empathetic identification," in which one puts oneself in the other's place, has enjoyed positive responses.[11] However, this model, Shildrick claims, remains within the binary opposition of self versus other (even if the self is here seen as relating to the other). It thus allows the other to be consumed by the self: the self remains the seer, who has expository agency, who recognizes the other as other, and as vulnerable. In Shildrick's work, the idea of vulnerability as wholly belonging to the other – the wimp or the wretched – is challenged, and in being challenged the issue is brought to bear on the precarious relationship, the interdependency, between self and other.[12] The encounter with vulnerability initiates an openness to the

---

11 See more on the notion of "empathetic identification" in Boler 1997: 260. There have been many attempts by feminist theorists to challenge a masculinist notion of ethics as developed by Immanuel Kant, John Rawls, or John Stuart Mill, which are based on duty, justice, and compliance. The feminist counter-models develop instead an ethics based on care, empathy, or trust. See for example Gilligan's "ethics of care" (1982). These ethical formulations have again been critically rethought by other feminist theorists who contend that there is a need for a dialogic ethics that does not privilege the standpoint of the caregiver over the cared-for, but respects the view of the other by giving it an emancipated voice. See more on the latter model in Koehn 1998.

12 Boler calls such a response "testimonial reading." She compares it also to Aristotle's conception of pity and Martha Nussbaum's notion of compassion. She states: "The central strategy of Aristotelian pity is a faith in the value of 'putting oneself in the other person's shoes'. By imagining my own similar vulnerabilities I claim 'I know what you are feeling because I fear that could happen to me'. The agent of empathy, then, is a fear for oneself. This signals the first risk of empathy: Aristotle's pity is more a story and projection of myself than an understanding of you" (Boler 1997: 257). Empathy can certainly be more than pity or compassion. To critically reconsider notions of empathy, compassion, or pity it might be useful to reflect on the concepts of affect and shame. See Tomkins 1963 and Sedgwick 2003.

unknown, to the strange or even the monstrous, that is an openness to the self's own vulnerability. This approach to vulnerability, according to Shildrick, "acknowledges both that the self and the other are mutually engaged, and yet are irreducible the one to the other" (ibid: 222).

I feel that Hoghe has attempted to create such a mutual engagement, against all odds of the theatre setting, which commonly present a one-sided engagement between actor and audience; the stage serving not only as the location for the spectacle, but also as a spatial and ideological boundary between performer and spectator. Hoghe's body is different not only from the bodies of his mostly able-bodied audience, but even more so from the classical ideal of a dancer's physique. He thus occupies one of the positions of radical corporeal otherness and seizes the stage as an intruder into the normative site of the theatre. He not only embodies the other as self (his corporeal nonconformity performs the role of a vulnerable subject-self), but he throws the audience's gaze back at them by refusing to occupy the demarcated reverse location, the negative side, of their selves.

We particularly see this happening in one scene of *Throwing the Body into the Fight*. Hoghe moves on stage from left to right, progressing slowly like a crab in the sand, his bare back turned towards his audience, with lights highlighting his deformed spine and white skin. Bearing in one hand a red chopstick, pointed at one end, Hoghe then draws an invisible line on his back, a curve, suggesting a smile, growing more apparent with each new stroke, as if it were being painted with lipstick (Fig. 2). But then this magic wand gets stuck on the uneven surface of Hoghe's back. The skin wrinkles, reddens, and stands out against the fair-skinned back. The hump and the asymmetrical proportions of Hoghe's body, his precise but fragile and carefully placed steps from left to right, his bare back, as well as his hidden face – all of these impressions now unsettle the viewer. How to look at him? Where to look?

Fig. 2: Screenshot from augen blicke N [Raimund Hoghe]

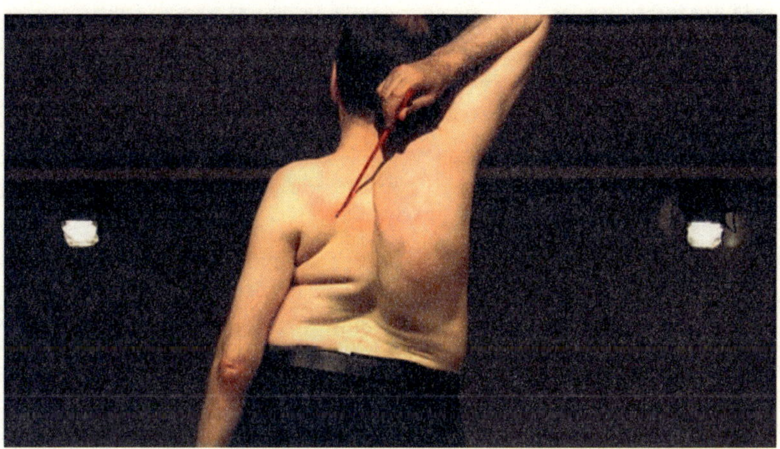

Source: Gitta Gsell (2005)

The stick that leaves a red mark on Hoghe's back draws the viewer's look to the part of his body that is usually draped in clothing, the spot at which one is enticed to stare. Yet, when prompted by self-consciousness or the gaze of others, one shamefully looks away from it. In the scene, Hoghe's performance compels his audience to *only* look at his back, since there is nothing else to see. He thus also gives his viewer the permission to stare, to look at his deformation without eliciting shame, disgust, or rejection. The red stick's stroking of the skin not only leaves a mark on Hoghe's body but almost physically responds to the viewer's reactions to the skin, recalling the familiar feeling of repetitive touch, ranging in sensation from pleasurable to soothing to irritating to painful. Watching Hoghe's skin turn nearly crimson, the viewer "sees" how it feels, and so comes to share the experience of his tender, sore, burning skin. This experience of vulnerable flesh opens up something in the viewer's vision. Hoghe's performance causes a synaesthetic perception in the viewer, in which the sensory experience of vision corresponds to or intermingles with the sensory experience of touch. This staged simultaneity of multiple sense-perceptions brings to the fore the limitations of "pure" vision and aims to dissolve the boundaries between the senses, as well as between seer and seen.[13]

---

13 See Bleeker 2008 on synaesthetic processes in the theatre.

Hoghe accompanies his dance work with thoughts on the effects of his performances:

People go to see dance theatre so as to identify with a beautiful, flawless body. With my body there is no such identification. People don't want to have my body. ... And, where does identification then take place? [As viewer] I can only look inwards; I am thrown back onto myself. People do not, in fact, see *me*, but they see something in themselves. (emphasis added)

The observation refers to what Mitchell observes in the encounter with disabled bodies where vision is momentarily threatened or blinded by the look of "the other," and where Hoghe's *me* is not seen. Hoghe productively uses this visual blindness and directs the audience's look back at them, so that they see something in themselves. He also redirects the everyday gaze onto the disabled body, a gaze that simply sees the other as third person, as exposed object.[14] In the viewing situation of the performance, the gazes of the audience similarly do not see Hoghe's *me*; instead of seeing his body as the object on display, they see their own first-person involvement in the act of viewing him on stage: his body is exposed to their looks just as their looking is exposed by his body. Hoghe disables empathic identification with his body as vulnerable other, instead rendering or projecting his audience's vulnerable selves. He invalidates vulnerability as a feature of the othering that brings violence with it. Hence, Hoghe *enables* a dialogic relationship between his audience and himself.

Hoghe's staged critique in certain ways answers Shildrick's crucial question:

What would it mean in other words to address the issue of vulnerability not *without* recourse to normative standards, but with a critique that exposed not simply the limits set by the cultural specificity of normativity ... but more radically yet [revealed] that the dichotomous structure is itself unstable? (2002: 78)

Shildrick formulates a possible consequence of such a performance:

---

14 For more on the relation between first, second, and third person in the context of public exposure, see Bal 1996: 3-4, 165-94. In connection to gestures of exposure within theatre practices, see Bleeker in van den Dries.

One immediate effect would be to place less emphasis on vulnerability as the dependency of others, and more on the notion of vulnerability as the risk of ontological uncertainty for all of us. (2002: 78)

The performance of disabled bodies on stage, as shown by Hoghe, Gosling, or Versnel in *augen blicke N*, allows us a glimpse of the fragility of "normal" embodiment and identity. The three artists put this fragility on stage, not by referring to the vulnerable other, but by exposing it as part of their own subjectivities. They thus attempt a redefinition of how we might relate to vulnerability – not as an empathic, outward response to a weak other, but as a subjective, inward reaction to a frail self. Ethical relationality is here reconceptualized.

How does this conception of vulnerability help to formulate a specific *aesthetics* of vulnerability? More particularly, how can the disabled body, as the agent that reveals the precariousness of becoming human, help to challenge visual practices of othering?

A VULNERABLE AESTHETIC

To answer those questions, I want to examine further the implications of risk as it has emerged from my discussion of theoretical approaches to visuality, vulnerability, and corporeality. With the help of a (counter)example, which combines disabled embodiment, visual art, and public exposure, I aim to see how risk helps us consider vulnerability as enabling certain visual practices. I want to discuss a controversial artwork by Marc Quinn, *Alison Lapper Pregnant* (Fig. 3).[15] A marble sculpture more than three meters tall, it portrays the artist Alison Lapper, showing her nude and eight-months pregnant. It was on display in London for eighteen months (September 2005–April 2007) on Trafalgar Square's fourth Plinth.

---

15 *Alison Lapper Pregnant* by Marc Quinn was unveiled on September 15, 2005, in London's Trafalgar Square.

Fig. 3: Alison Lapper Pregnant

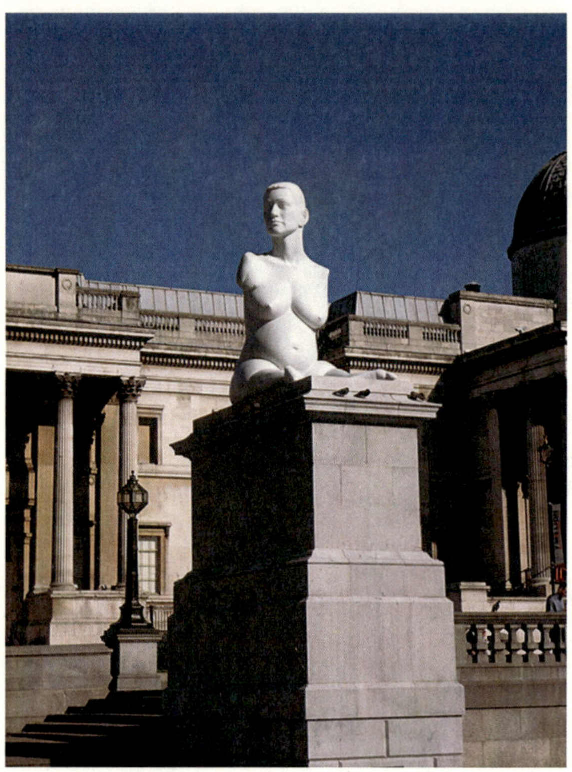

Source: Marc Quinn (2005), photograph Marc Quinn Studio

Quinn's sculpture, positioned in London's crowded center alongside equestrian statues of such heroes of the British Empire as Lord Nelson, shows a self-confident, almost warrior-like woman, who suffers from phocomelia, a congenital condition that caused her to be born with shortened legs and without arms or hands. Cast as a statue in sleek white Italian marble, Lapper is depicted as a mother-to-be with a disabled body. The work caused some controversy: the statue was said to be powerful and inspiring as well as ugly and repellent. It elicits shamed yet fascinated reactions to the pregnant woman's nakedness along with feelings of empowerment for people with disabilities. Alison Lapper's own art aims to put disability, femininity, and motherhood on the map of public recognition.[16] But does this representation of her as a disabled maternal subject manage to destabilize conventional aesthetic ideals and challenge ways of looking at disabled bodies in public?

Alison Lapper Pregnant certainly activates a public discourse and represents disability in a positive and visible way. It does not, however, provoke or facilitate a dialogue between viewer and visual object, between outward and inward looking, because it does not return the viewer's gaze back to its sender. The immense sculpture triggers ideological unease in its references to femininity and motherhood: pregnancy in women with disabilities challenges common assumptions that disabled people are asexual. Additionally, good motherhood has traditionally been regarded as the preserve of the healthy, strong, and beautiful, whose virtues would benefit the continuance of the human race. But while maternity has been seen as the salvation of latently unruly women, pregnancy, regarded as one of the most embodied and least comprehensible experiences, has nonetheless been closely tied to the monstrous.

Shildrick brings to the fore two main cultural conceptions that connect the maternal body with the monstrous: the "deformatory power" of maternal imagination and the monstrosity of the maternal body itself. Both notions are built upon anxieties about human origins and corporeal borders; a body that incubates, unseen, within itself another body disrupts normative conceptualizations of the body. The idea of maternal imagination assumes a mother's capacity to produce a deformed, disabled, in-human or soul-less fetus by the workings of imagination. The monstrosity of the maternal body itself relates to the cultural notion of a clean and proper self, which is challenged by the two lives' symbiosis during pregnancy and early childhood. The mother is thus not only capable of producing monsters, but embodies monstrosity herself (2002: 41).

In an essay on the monstrous as a potential site of agency in visual art on the disabled maternal body, Rosemary Betterton observes:

---

16 Lapper, mainly working with painting, photography, and digital imaging, questions physical normality and established conceptions of what counts as beautiful.

In our own biomedical times, miscarriages and birth malformations are routinely ascribed to maternal ill health or genetics, but to our early modern forebears, "monstrous" births were products of a powerful maternal imagination …. (2006: 81)

Alison Lapper, visibly deformed, evokes, as expectant mother, a predictable anxiety about reproductive rights, and disturbs notions of femininity, humanness, and proper embodiment. Quinn's sculpture consequently helps to disrupt not only maternal ideals, but also the ways we look at disabled bodies.

In this respect, *Alison Lapper Pregnant* serves as a good example to show different modes of embodiment. Nevertheless, the gleaming marble statue absorbs rather than reflects the gazes directed towards it, whether in awe or in shock. It is simply too heroic to imagine it to be disturbed by injurious looks or to blush when admired. *Alison Lapper Pregnant* does not, in my eyes, account for vision's blindness to the specific difference of disabled embodiment, which cannot become visible under the confining aesthetic regimes of beauty and perfection. Despite the material presence of the stone sculpture, one observes only a fixed and paradoxically dematerialized pregnant subject with severe limb disabilities. Betterton supports this view when she writes, "The choice of marble has the effect of stabilizing the potentially disruptive figure of the disabled pregnant mother, whose embodiment is immobilized in memorial form" (86).

The stabilizing effect of the artwork's surface quality enforces a seeming accuracy of vision, while vision itself, as Mitchell claims, being under the constant threat of blindness, fails to see the complex (social and political) embodiment behind the clean façade. Unquestionably, the sculpture challenges conventional views of disabled bodies and motherhood, and claims some public recognition of the social existence of unruly bodies. But at the same time, the artwork seems to preclude, or even shy away from, reference to these bodies' unruliness and their specific corporeality and intimacy. In the encounter with the marbled beauty on Trafalgar Square, embodied experience remains silent, untouched, untouchable.

Based on my argument here, one might ask if such a dis-embodied experience must not be true for every stone sculpture, stone being a cold and hard material. I would not think so, as not every marble sculpture aestheticizes the body the way Quinn's does. And the material itself is not the only determining factor in how a figure is perceived. Form, color, texture, size, light, expression, surrounding atmosphere, and installation of the artwork are, in my eyes, as decisive for a viewer's perception as the material itself. If Quinn's artistic and critical tool is the aestheticization of the disruptive body, independent of the chosen materiality, it also has its downside, which is its antagonism to aliveness, sensuality, and embodiedness.

In Bal's discussion of the object of visual studies, she ascribes to specific artworks the potential to "mobilize art for an *embodied reflection* on [elements of visual culture that do not belong to the traditional domain of art]" (2005: 153; emphasis in original). Although Bal's critique is specifically aimed at the field of visual studies, I claim that her observation generally broaches the subject of an artwork's material involvement in the process of visual perception. Art that motivates embodied reflection, or involved looking, not only inaugurates an ethically valuable form of looking – by appealing to the viewer's responsibility in the creation of the image – but it also makes room for the visual object's agency in the perceived image. With such mutual involvement between viewer and object, another element comes into play: the risk, not of vision itself, as we saw in Mitchell, but of the encounter with the other. This risk of looking at the other also involves *being seen by* the other, which adds to the act of looking the awareness that one always looks from a contingent ontological position. Consequently, the awareness of one's positional and thus perspectival viewpoint toward the other threatens the ostensibly objective and unidirectional way of knowing what one sees.[17]

Finally, I want to question how the artistic performances of the dancers in *augen blicke N* differ from Quinn's sculpture. I hope to have shown that *Alison Lapper Pregnant* challenges common modes of looking, which pathologize and immobilize people with disabilities. The figure achieves this goal by showing self-confidence, empowerment, and a certain condescension towards those who have seen in her the "monstrous (m)other." In contrast to this mode of visuality, Hoghe and the other dancers in *augen blicke N* develop new modes of looking at bodies. They

---

17 See Bal on the notion of historical looking, which includes the awareness of the problematic of looking at/from the vantages of gender, color, physical disposition. 1996: 286.

all show their particular experiences of vulnerability in light of the categorizing and often injurious looks with which they are confronted every day. In this respect, I see a significant disparity between *Alison Lapper Pregnant* and *augen blicke N*: whereas the former shows resistance and force, the latter shows vulnerability.

It seems that risking one's corporeal wholeness and inner untouchability by showing oneself as a vulnerable being is one of the conditions for a potentially unstable, transformative, and fragile aesthetic. Here we come to an aesthetic conception that allows us to look differently at non-normative embodiment, being responsive to the other's experience as well as to one's own susceptibility to difference. When Shildrick criticizes that we "still see our bodies almost as though they were suits of armour protecting a core self" (2000: 221), she touches on the core of conventional ways of seeing the other and of being looked at by disruptively embodied selves. Encounters like those with the performances of Hoghe, Gosling, and Versnel open up latent fissures in the protective shield of their viewers' bodies. The normal-bodied viewer becomes vulnerable to her or his (dialogic) vision of the differently-bodied other. Hoghe symbolically demonstrates the process when he takes off his plaster cast. On the one hand, it protects him from the looks of others at his disabled body; on the other, it insinuates that he bears a heavy burden on his shoulders. Hoghe shows that the protective armor, which, more than able-bodied subjects, he has used to protect himself against injurious looks, can be taken off, showing a particular vulnerability to being looked at. The body as protective covering thus becomes the very accessory of an aesthetic of beauty and intangibility, which reveals one's self as dependent on and vulnerable to the other.

Shildrick's call for an *ethics of risk* is a necessary step towards an aesthetic of vulnerability:

The notion of an irreducible vulnerability as the necessary condition of a fully corporeal becoming – of myself and always *with* others – shatters the ideal of the self's clean and proper body; and it calls finally for the willingness to engage in an ethics of risk. (2002: 86; emphasis added)

For the dancers in *augen blicke N*, embodying vulnerability in the theatre is a mode of exposing themselves and their audience to the risks as well as the enablement of regarding (observing and respecting) other bodies in relation to one's own embodiment. Seeing disability for the audience develops into seeing enablement. Gazing at the other becomes glancing at oneself. What happens between viewer and seen can then be described as an aesthetic practice that is linked to an ethics of becoming human, an ethics that links the self to the other: an ethics that commits to encountering the former monster.

The implications of such a potentially risky ethics of vision motivate me, in the following chapter, to question the ability of visual self-representation to represent queer selves. I will explore the relationship between the formation of self and self-imaging. I look at how a certain loss of self in self-portraits not only exposes the failure of visual representation to fully portray a subject, but that this loss of self can be productive for imperfect, gender-ambiguous, and queer subjects to expose their subjectivity beyond commonly projected identities.

Portraiture and Self-Loss

Fig. 4: Que me veux-tu?

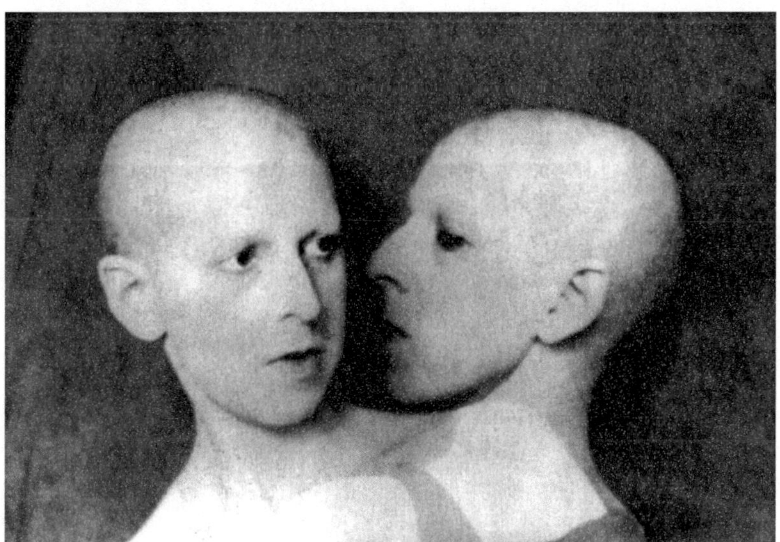

Source: Claude Cahun (1929), Musée d'Art Moderne de la Ville de Paris

Two twin-like bald heads, both with small dark eyes and mouths, theatrically present themselves to the viewer of a black-and-white photograph (1929) by the French artist Claude Cahun (Fig. 4). These sets of eyes and mouths are engaged in a visual dialogue, involving each other and possibly someone standing in front of the image. The heads twist toward each other at an angle: they bend uncomfortably backwards or sideways to avoid touching each other with their noses or cheeks. Though conjoined at their upper shoulders, like Siamese twins, each expresses a kind of independence in their postures, contradicting their cloned appearance. As defiant as they seem toward each other, there is little space in the image for the one head to avoid the other. As a result, they come across as identical doubles who nonetheless exhibit disparate personalities.

Caught in the frame of the photograph, the starkly lit white heads are positioned against a diffuse grey background that, with its faint grid-like pattern of straight lines, intensifies the contrast between the image's rectangular form and the subjects' rounded scalps. The pair looks involuntarily trapped in the constricted space of a photographic print. The doubleness of the faces and the work's title intensify this impression by suggesting that each investigates the presence of the other in the image. *Que me veux-tu?* asks: What do you want from me?[1] Denying each other's claim to be represented exclusively, the two subjects highlight the struggle of each for recognition. Caught in space, they seem, however, to break the spell of time: the photographic process has frozen the movements of eyes and mouths, but the recorded moment is so expressive that it draws the viewer into a continuing exchange of looks; an exchange that transcends the still space of the image and builds a relation to the spectator.

The twins do not struggle for each other's recognition – the two sets of eyes do not clearly look *at* one another – but for the sort of social recognition that Judith Butler describes in her account of social address, where an individual's social recognition is dependent on the address of the other or on the interpellation of a self by the other, as when someone says, "Hey you!" (Butler 1997: 5). This account of recognition simultaneously declares its possible failure and the addressed subject's lack of will. On a

---

1 Nathanaël Stephens kindly brought to my attention that Cahun used this photograph as a model for a drawing on the cover of a novel by Georges Ribemont-Dessaignes, *Frontières Humaines* (1929). The title accompanying the drawing reads: "N'ayez pas peur d'etre dévorés" (Do not fear being devoured). In contrast to the photograph's title, the drawing does not pose a question and consequently does not clearly state who is speaking: the plural might intend to address a multitude of viewers as well as the two represented subjects in the image. This confusion, paired with the pretended reassurance in the statement – which of course has the contrary effect – points to Cahun's play with forms of (self-)representation and social address.

visual level, I interpret self-portraiture as a form of representation that calls for recognition by the viewer, a form of address that calls on the other to recognize the portrayed, to hail the depicted subject into social existence. In that sense, self-portraiture counteracts the initial "lack of will" inherent in being addressed, while adhering to and even buying into the common norms of recognition. In Cahun's double portrait, the call for recognition might be seen as a double counteraction in that it actively prompts an address from the viewer (What do you want?) and confuses her form of address (Who – one, two, male, female – is there to be addressed?).

The composition of the photograph bears resemblance to an early Greek form of "naturalistic portraiture," which took the form of double busts.[2] "Double herms" date back to the early first century B.C.E. The sculptures usually consist of two heads conjoined at their back from crown to neck and shoulder. They were commonly mounted on pillars marking the entrance of a house or the boundary between two streets, rooms, or fields.[3] The faces often represent two closely related, yet different figures of historical or intellectual importance. Cahun's image makes patent reference to the idea of the double herm, yet mocks it too, by apparently displaying the "same" face twice and by turning the faces toward each other, which creates a space and a border *within* the sculpture instead of marking an external spatial border.

I read Cahun's self-portrait as a classical double portrait with a twist: it stages two subjects made alike, not through garments, make-up, headdress, posture, or other identifiable accessories, but through the absence of markers of identity. Cahun's image is stripped of details that would link the portrayed subjects to the outside world. Because there are no references to where, when, and under what conditions this photograph was taken, the faces are presented to their viewers with a commanding directness. The brightly lit skin enhances the effect of bareness, highlighting the absence of clothing or other adornment, behind which the portrayed could have hidden themselves. The harsh light paradoxically obfuscates meaningful details in

---

2 Joanna Woodall describes "naturalistic portraiture" as an attempt to represent the identity of the depicted subject through physiognomic likeness. She refers to the early twentieth-century artists' challenge to the idea that visual resemblance necessarily represents a model's identity (Woodall 1997: 8).

3 For more on ancient Greek portrait sculpture, see Dillon 2006.

the subjects' faces. It is impossible to see personalizing signs, such as wrinkles, pimples, or birthmarks, and it is difficult even to make out the exact forms of ears, chins, mouths, and noses. Likewise the undefined, geometric background, disturbed only by the two blotches of dark shadow created by the heads, offers scant information about the setting of the image.

To me, the image defies the identificatory power of representation in portraits. It performs a critique of portraiture, and especially of the possibility that photography can capture subjectivity. I view the image as a precarious mirror image, not of the artist and her subjectivity, but of the complexity and obscurity of visual (self-)representation.

A 1995 painting by Catalan artist Miquel Barceló, *Double Portrait (anverso de Deux Papayes)* (Fig. 5), exhibits similar themes, while also showing meaningful differences.

Fig. 5: Double Portrait (anverso de Deux Papayes)

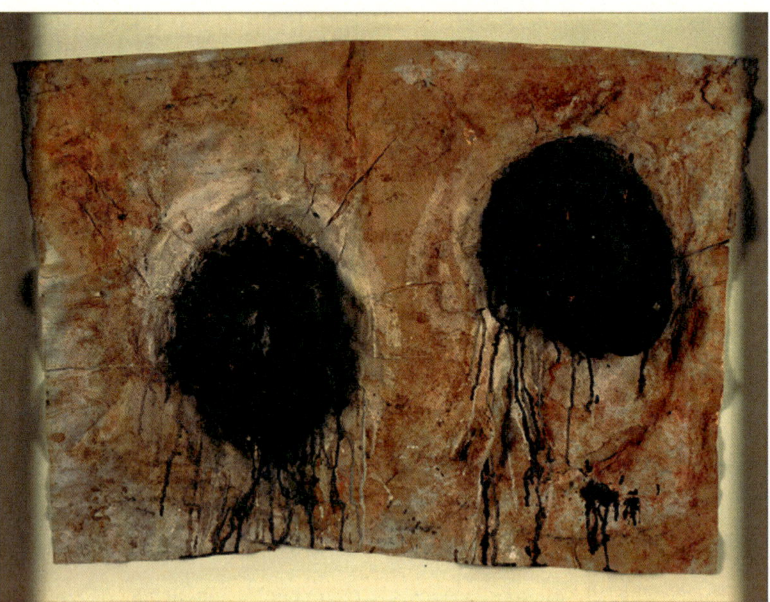

Source: Miquel Barceló (1995), Musée national d'art moderne / Centre de création industrielle

In Barceló's painting, two dark-colored heads stand out against a light-colored background. The heads are neckless and hairless, and lack clear indications of eyes, mouths, or noses. These face-shaped, yet blurry forms could almost be seen as two halves of an oval fruit-like object, as is indeed suggested by the title's reference to the image on the verso, entitled *Deux Papayes*. To call Barceló's image a portrait seems macabre: the heads are depicted as melting ovoids of black against a beige and white background. To perceive the two black lumps as faces is suggestive, yet painful in view of their decaying state. The heads maintain a subject- as well as an object-position for the viewer and confuse, as does Cahun's image, the point of reference for the portrayed subject(s).

In Cahun's and Barceló's images, the color effects and atmospherics employed guide us to see the paired heads of each in a particular fashion. While the exposed and vulnerable-looking faces of Cahun emphasize the subjects' potentially more feminine markers such as rounded chins, missing facial hair, or narrow shoulders, Barcelo's rough and dark faces evoke racialized stereotypes associated with dark skin, such as full lips, large ears, or "nappy hair."

The most revealing difference between Barceló's painting and Cahun's photograph is the reversed color scheme and the respective visibility or invisibility of the heads' eyes and looks. Cahun's two faces are almost blinding against the image's background. The multiple eyes and mouths stand out starkly, leaving the impression of piercing looks and cavernous throats. In contrast, Barceló's heads are black against ocher, and are adorned with halo-like white illuminations. The eyes and mouths are barely visible; indeed, one suspects rather than sees them. Only the form and tilt of the vestigial heads suggest that the head on the right looks to the right, while the other looks straight ahead. Barceló's double portrait amasses color and form in such a way that the two faces become black holes resembling hollow eyes. What becomes of the portrayed subjects in the image? Where do the selves of the depicted faces reside?

What in Cahun's image is over-lit is, in Barceló's image, under-lit. Yet both have a similar effect: the obliteration of human features that would allow the viewer to determine the subjects' gender, race, and age, and possibly their societal or cultural origins. As a result, the heads become removed from the category of the human. The missing reference to an original subject in the portrait through doubling and cloning is reinforced by the use of lighting and the play with the contrast between black and white.

This contrast, especially when comparing the two images, suggests a further difference between Cahun and Barceló. While Cahun's faces are dominated by the small but piercing black holes of their eyes and mouths, Barceló's faces appeal, through the lack of light, to the viewer's imagination and call on her to fill in what is denied to vision. Despite this difference, I contend that both images suggest that what becomes meaningful in the representation of subjectivity is precisely what the viewer *cannot* see.

Against the background of this challenge to visibility, I would like to explore the intricacies of knowing oneself through representation. Cahun's and Barceló's images suggest that subjectivity is formed, yet also *de*-formed, through portraiture. Artistic self-representations that explore queer forms of identification offer ways of analyzing the deformed or transformed self in visuality. With the phrase "queer identification" I want to describe forms of identification that challenge the stability of identity and question the formation of subjectivity through linear and socially invariable processes. Queerness here stands more for the dislocation or the disturbance of representational traditions, linked to heteronormative ideals of gender and sexuality, than for the particular artists' sexual orientation. Queer self-representations allow us to positively rethink the formation of subjectivity within the field of vision. My aim is to reveal a certain productivity that emerges from the loss of self in queer portraiture.

In order to substantiate this claim, I first examine psychoanalytical and phenomenological theories of subject-formation and their conception of narcissism, which, in relation to Cahun's artwork, challenge the belief in the self's containment and uniqueness.[4] The self is analyzed in its amorous but potentially uneasy relation to itself. But then, in my own theoretical double portrait, I will approach portraiture from a different direction. I contextualize Cahun's image and a self-portrait by British-American artist

---

4 Cahun's double images recur throughout her oeuvre and additionally allude to an emphasis on self-perception and self-awareness. They also suggest her struggles with narcissism, which, Danielle Knafo observes, "found a suitable stage in her art. She once wrote, 'Narcissism? Of course. It is my best feature'" (2001: 45).

Del LaGrace Volcano (*Andro Del*, 2005). Volcano's photograph cites, yet opposes, the gaze leveled at gender-deviant subjects in scientific portrait photographs. Volcano's portrait reverses the hostility of the scientific photographs to their sitters as well as the "flattering" portrayal shown in narcissistic representations. Both Cahun and Volcano combine these two opposed traditions of portraiture, countering the ways that these traditions have produced subjectivity. Thus, the scientifically studied self comes to play a subversive role in queer art works. I will turn here to the question of how a self can (re)present itself to others. Following Judith Butler's conception of giving an account of oneself in language, I suggest that Cahun and Volcano, by challenging portraiture's normative condition of likeness, defy regimes of gender, race, and age. In so doing, they allow us to consider possible alternative forms of communicating subjectivity in the field of visuality.

NARCISSUS AND THE LOSS OF SELF

> Le corps de Narcisse se vide et se perd
> Dans l'abîme de son reflet[.]
> SALVADOR DALÍ[5]

Recounting Ovid's version of the Narcissus legend, Mieke Bal illustrates the occurrence of a "hidden" life in the image:

This story of "death and the image" is about the denial of the true, natural body, not as opposed to, but as inhering in, the body's image. The point is not that the body "behind" what we see can be revealed in its reality. The point is that there is a "real" body inside the image, which is – precisely because it is inside – out of reach, of vision. (1999: 238)

---

5   "The body of Narcissus flows out and loses itself / In the abyss of his reflection[.]"

For Narcissus, what is fatal is not excessive self-love, as common interpretations of the myth have suggested, but a sense of hopelessness that is triggered as he loses his self to the assumed lover and his real body to its image. The loss of Narcissus's self to his mirror image as love object leads to his death or, more poetically, to his transformation into a flower.

Dying is intricately bound up in Narcissus's relationship to his reflection. Desiring his specular image, Narcissus falls prey to the very condition of becoming a human subject, as Freud and Lacan have theorized in different ways.[6] Freud interprets the myth as a symbol for a self-absorbed subject whose libido is directed more toward his own ego than toward other subjects. While Freud believes that narcissism can lead to a form of perversion or disorder, he also argues that narcissism reflects a stage in every subject's psychosexual development: "primary narcissism" designates a necessary stage between auto-eroticism and object-love. The child's libidinal attachment to her mirror image allows the subject to acquire a sense of self and humanness (1989). The subject's (ideally) intermediary state of self-love symbolizes Narcissus's imaginary death. The realization that his desire can never be satisfied is accompanied by the recognition that he will have to leave behind his self.

Lacan similarly draws on the myth as the model for human subjectivity and death. Freud's formulation of primary narcissism is recast by Lacan as a process whereby relationships are internalized – first the child's relationship to itself, and later the subject's relationship to others. In his 1949 essay on the "mirror stage," *stade du miroir*, as well as in later rearticulations of his thesis, he radicalizes Freud's account by characterizing the subject's formation in the mirror stage as a simultaneous alienation from itself. In the mirror stage, the child forms an ego through an imaginary projection, believed to be the external reflection in the mirror, which is its counterpart, its non-self. Narcissism is caused by the self's identifications with the images and language that convey the seeming consistency of a bodily entity that, however, is situated at some remove from the subject's body. In the mirror stage, identification with one's image

---

6   Freud elaborates the reference to the mythical youth in love with his reflection
    for the first time in 1915 in "Three Essays on the Theory of Sexuality." He
    develops his theory of narcissism in his 1914 essay "On Narcissism." See also
    Lacan 1968.

creates a corporeal image that partly replaces the child's corporeal experience. Narcissus's recognition of himself as a desirable object in the image is accompanied by the loss of his bodily self/life.[7] Becoming-subject through a visual process leads to a failure to survive humanness.

For Lacan, the reflection of the subject in her self-image demonstrates a particular power: on the one hand, it establishes an erotic relation between self and self-image; on the other hand, it alienates the subject by placing the ego in the mirror, thus creating a split between outer appearance and inner reality. In the mirror, the child recognizes its body as an image (an external *Gestalt*), which presents an apparent unity and wholeness that is objectively missing from the child's body-image (inner experience). The mirror image consequently triggers a form of identification that the subject experiences as external to the self. Ultimately, the mirror stage paradoxically is alienating even as it serves as a means for self-discovery. It constitutes a subject by way of self-love and self-loss simultaneously.

In his book on Lacan, Malcolm Bowie (1993) writes: "The 'alienating destination' of the 'I' is such that the individual is permanently in discord with himself" (25). The self's inner discord leads to an identification, which removes the self from itself but that is preferably overcome by the simultaneous desire for and identification with others. In this sense, narcissism, as formulated by Lacan, is necessary to becoming a subject insofar as it establishes a relation between the subject's *Innenwelt* (organism) and *Umwelt* (surrounding reality) (Lacan 2006: 78). At the same time, it is a drama in which the self is split between a body-image and an alienated identity – a drama that transforms the self from what Lacan calls the "specular *I*" into the "social *I*" (ibid: 79).

In seeming contrast to traditional and psychoanalytical interpretations of the story, Maurice Merleau-Ponty's phenomenology adds another dimension to our understanding of narcissism. Merleau-Ponty observes a fundamental narcissism in all vision, and ascribes to narcissistic behavior a positive and socially constructive element (1968: 139). Humanity and identity are conditioned by the visual reciprocity of self and others, which is elicited by the body's sensual interaction with the surrounding world.

---

7   The version of the myth that has Narcissus transformed into a daffodil (narcissus) seems to attest to the loss of human life while allowing for the continuation of life in a different, subject-less, form.

Self-seeing establishes a necessary "intercorporeity" between the subject and others (141). The objects seen return the subject's look and constitute the subject's being in the world. Feeling oneself looked at becomes an experience comparable to the reciprocity of touch, through which a hand that touches something equally feels the touch of the object.

Vision constitutes the subject as part of the human landscape. This characterization of vision as an almost material condition represents for Merleau-Ponty a necessary element for subjectivity, formed always in relation to other subjects and the material world. As strongly as Freud's and Lacan's accounts of narcissism introduce a sense of identity that separates the subject from the maternal body and the world of others, Merleau-Ponty stresses the foundational character of vision in the constitution of the self vis-à-vis other subjects. The boundary of the child's skin that separates her from the rest of the physical world, so important in psychoanalysis for the formation of the self, in phenomenology facilitates the physical and mental interaction with others. Lacan's alienation is turned into the necessary element for becoming a social human subject.

Merleau-Ponty posits the quest for the unity of the self as a communicative task: engagement with the surrounding world through the receptivity and reciprocity of the body. [8] In his essay "Visions of Narcissism" (1991), David Michael Levin interprets Merleau-Ponty's "narcissism of the flesh" in a way that radically reverses pathological definitions of "narcissistic personality disorder," especially in Freud and later psychiatric conceptions:

In [Merleau-Ponty's] "narcissism" of the flesh, there is ... a dialectic of reflection, and this dialectic deconstructs the narcissistic structure of the self, redeeming, at the very heart of "subjectivity", its primordial sociality, its inherence in the reciprocities of a social world ... (54)

If self-reflection is reciprocated by another subject rather than by a lifeless mirror, it returns a different image, which potentially shows more of the other than merely one's imagined self. In other words, the self is reflected *in*, but also *through*, another subject. The reflection of the self becomes a

---

8   For more on Merleau-Ponty's "hermeneutics of the flesh" and his "phenomeno-logy of narcissism," see Levin 1991: 53-54.

matter of who is reflecting whom.[9] Where is the subject ultimately formed: in the reflected image or in the space between self and other?

Unlike Lacan, Merleau-Ponty situates the facilitating specular image in the body of the other.[10] While for Lacan the transformative character of self-reflection depends on the gaze of the (m)other who sees the self seeing itself in the mirror, for Merleau-Ponty the process of seeing oneself reflected in the other lies in the reciprocity of a shared vision. Seeing one another seeing, in this sense, does not answer to a psychoanalytic formulation of ego-formation, but reveals the productive dimension of vision, which allows for a reciprocal view of the self as shaped by the presence of the other.[11] This "mirror of flesh" suggests not only a basic interaction between the self and others through the body, but also predicates the self's fundamental otherness. The self-alienation that Lacan ascribes is here not so much a *méconnaissance* (illusionary or false recognition) but rather an extended recognition: a recognition enlarged by the aspects of the other's features in the flesh. The self is thus defined by its own decentered, yet not fragmented, body and by the bodies of others. As a consequence, the partial loss of self in narcissistic processes of identification is now positively connoted, since it is constructive for every subject's sociality.

In his book on visual representation in the Western tradition, Stephen Bann calls the relation between Narcissus and his reflection "specular reciprocity" (1989: 133). Bann situates the dependency between portrayed subject and outside spectator on a second level. In typical artistic representations, Narcissus observes himself in his reflection, so that the viewer of the work participates in an act of voyeurism (ibid: 128). When Bann connects art's historical preoccupation with the myth of Narcissus to more recent painting and photography, he observes a fundamental shift in the relation to images of self-reflection or self-projection as experienced by artists and spectators alike. These artists and viewers of art, Bann contends,

---

9   Bal in Bal and Bryson 2001: 246.

10 Levin's essay shows Lacan's influence on Merleau-Ponty's phenomenology, yet presents the fundamental differences between the two approaches to the formation of the subject.

11 Merleau-Ponty calls the flesh a mirror phenomenon and, alluding to Lacan's glass mirror, sees it as the formative medium of the subject and the object.

are confronted with an amended form of narcissism, in which Narcissus is saved from the fatal spiral of self-reflection by interiorizing the effect of representation.[12]

Taking this interiorization into account means that, for a number of Western artists, self-portraits are more truthful than their real selves (Paul Klee), images of self and other converge or shift (Paul Cézanne), or an inner sense of self, a sense of wholeness, is projected outwards onto the picture plane, toward an outside viewer (William Tucker) (ibid: 166, 185, 181). Bann further observes that the photographic medium, which is experienced through its shiny, coated prints, can evoke the surface of Narcissus's pool of water. Hence, the emergence of photography symbolically challenged the myth of Narcissus. Instead of situating pictorial signification within the image, it now pertains to the materiality of the picture's very surface. Traditionally, "Narcissus is trapped in the specular unity of the self and its image," writes Bann (ibid: 154). The self remains within the image, voyeuristically contemplated by an outside spectator. Later, as the visual history of the myth suggests, the self is also represented in and by the medium or the materiality of the image, thus standing in a closer and possibly more involved relation to the spectator. One might even suggest that the specular (mirroring) reciprocity of Narcissus and his reflection have been transposed to a visual (viewing) reciprocity of self and other. In a sense, then, Merleau-Ponty's narcissism of the flesh has already been put into practice by contemporary artists, who question a subject's relation to their visual representation.

If, then, in earlier artworks, Narcissus and his reflection often mirrored each other, later the "perfect" likeness of the two versions of Narcissus was distorted. Cahun plays with such likeness by showing a clear resemblance between the two faces, while twisting their poses and bestowing each with distinct gazes. The one face is not like the other; they are two selves, not

---

12 In reference to Leon Baptista Alberti's art theory, Stephen Bann gives a detailed account of how the story of Narcissus became a keystone in the history of the visual arts. While Alberti contends that Narcissus was "the inventor of painting," Bann cautions us to remember that Narcissus, after all, was not an artist but a hunter. Nevertheless, Bann states that the Narcissus myth has had profound consequences for the history of representation in the broadest sense (Bann 1989: 105-6).

two images of a single self. Cahun's critical revision of likeness establishes a crucial connection to the different theories of narcissism I have presented above. Art, in opposition to theory, thus adds to the analysis of narcissism an important aspect that lies in the image itself. Specifically, because of photography's historical connection to likeness, Cahun's image can manifest itself, as I regard it here, as an example of a particular form of narcissism: a narcissism that leads to a loss of self.[13]

Cahun's dual portrait unavoidably invokes the theme of the double. Such doubling literalizes what Linda Nochlin describes as "the meeting of two subjectivities" in portraiture.[14] If, in the traditional portrait, the viewer is confronted with the portrayer and the portrayed, the self-portrait projects another double encounter: the meeting of two forms of subjectivity belonging to the same person, namely the artist and the artist's self-reflection. The simultaneous presence of self and self-image in the self-portrait gives way, in Cahun's photograph, to a dislocation of two versions of the same subject. Each of the two heads seems to have made space for the other's appearance in the image, which points not only to their doubled or split subjectivity, but also to a mutual recognition of each other's existence.[15]

Despite the likeness of the two faces, it remains unclear whether the two subjects are identical twins. If not twins, they can only be duplications of each other, and are thus one subject. The photograph presents the viewer with the conceptual problem of the *Doppelgänger*. The subject's ghostly double confuses the opposition between the original and the clone, elicits

---

13 For more on photographic portraiture and likeness, see Gage 1997.

14 From her 1974 essay "Some Women Realists"; quoted in van Alphen 2005: 21.

15 In an essay on Claude Cahun and the "third sex," Danielle Knafo emphasizes Cahun's preoccupation with the theme of the double in her artistic works. (46) Quoting Otto Rank who stated on the double motif that "The idea of death ... is denied by a duplication of the self" (Rank: 83), Knafo sees Cahun's double as a protective function against the loss of self: Should one self die or go mad, the second self would survive. This thesis reads Cahun's creation of a *Doppelgänger* as a mode of survival. In contrast, I interpret Cahun's double as a move *away* from the self – away from a stable, fixed, or normed self and toward a multitude of selves, which give the artist more freedom to become a person beyond traditional social categories.

an uncertainty that becomes more pronounced when we realize that the original is elsewhere and the depicted subjects are *both* replicas of Claude Cahun, the photographer. The title of the artwork adds to our bewilderment. It asks, provocatively, "What do you want from me?" without indicating who has posed the question, or to whom it is addressed. *Que me veux-tu?* can also be translated as "What do you want *with* me?" or as "How do I bother you?" The question in French has an old-fashioned structure, in which two grammatical objects (accusative *que* and indirect *me*) reside. The interrogative pronoun *what* and the personal pronoun *me* become confused; the meaning of the question is thus blurred. I want to suggest that Cahun chose this title so as to leave unclear who is posing the question and to whom it is directed. Cahun's image confronts the viewer with an exchange between an invisible original and its two similar, yet different copies. The doubling of the represented subject and its narcissistic self-imaging paradoxically meet in Cahun's photograph. The self-centered relation exhibited by the artist is multiplied and hence transformed into a plurality of narcissistic selves.

The theme of duplication refers to a fundamental condition of portraiture, which depends on the face being able to be reproduced in representation. Joanna Woodall suggests that "a portrait is a likeness which is seen to refer to the identity of the person depicted" (1997: 9-10). There is, however, another conception of portraiture that questions the conflation between person and representation. Embodying a dualist perspective on portraiture, this view posits a division between a person's living body and her true inner self. This means that likeness here forms a barrier between the sitter and the representation of her "real" self. Such a vantage, coupled with other conceptions of portraiture, allows me to interpret Cahun's image both as a self-identificatory examination of the artist and as an attempt to stress the distinction between identity and the material body.

To painting or to photograph a face is to double it, but also to bestow on that double an uncanny life of its own: the created image hovers between reality and fiction. The represented face must resemble the original closely enough to meet the expected conditions of portraiture, yet it must not be identical to the real so as not to threaten the subject's uniqueness. The fine line between these two requirements makes portraiture, on the one hand, a precarious mode of representation; on the other hand, the genre allows for experimentation with the critical nature of representation in relation to subjectivity and reality – and, as I want to argue, in relation to gender, race, and age. Cahun's double portrait, with its narcissistic dualism, combines a critical perspective on portraiture with a special conception of narcissistic identification.

The photograph refers to Lacan's mirror stage not only by showing two faces that appear to be mirror images of the other but also by exposing the faces' mutual acknowledgment. They seem to become who they are through seeing each other seeing, as well as through posing to be seen by a third viewer, the spectator. Lacan's narcissism is brought onto the picture plane. The inner formation of subjectivity is transposed into a process of entering into visual representation.

At the same time, the image does not use a real mirror but generates what Merleau-Ponty calls the mirror in the flesh: one face is mirrored in and through the other. The likeness given by a mirror is constituted here in the flesh of the other, eerily alike, yet clearly different. In that sense, Cahun presents a self that is defined through the other in the self's own flesh. *Que me veux-tu?* reflects Merleau-Ponty's idea of self-seeing as a condition for the relation to others by its creation of an intercorporeity between bodies. Because self and other become interchangeable, Merleau-Ponty's notion of a fundamental narcissism inherent in vision turns into the visual interaction between multiple selves, playing out in relation to an outside viewer. Self-reflection becomes, if not a social performance, then an interactive staging of self-formation. Lacan's and Merleau-Ponty's theories come together in Cahun's image, transformed into an expression of selfhood that sheds new light on self-portraiture and identification.

Reflecting on feminist art, Rosy Martin claims that self-portraiture "is a way of coming into representation for women, in which the artist is both subject and object and conceives of how she looks in the sense of how she sees rather than how she appears" (quoted in Meskimmon 1996: xv). The twofold and in this case facilitating structure of seeing and appearing (being seen), coupled with the synchrony of subject- and object-positions, relates to Cahun's work in a different way: the portrait is staged not so much for an outside viewer but rather for Cahun's own eyes. Her selves come into view for each other.

The confused object/subject- and personhood-status results in a qualification of originality and reference. Where in or for Cahun's image is the original situated? The two faces demonstrate the impossibility of a primary model, the real thing. Outside the image, one can hardly imagine another, a third self, serving as the original for both. Consequently, Cahun becomes a subject without referent inside or outside the image. She presents herself as the representation not of a unique individual, but of an unbound subjectivity. Presenting herself as duplicated, she stages a certain absence. Subjectivity is lost in the quest for it. Nonetheless, visually, both selves act like self-determined individuals, performing their personhood with confidence. Cahun's self-determination produces a form of subjectivity in which a core self is absent, lost, or given up. My larger aim in the present chapter is to unearth the potential productivity of this loss for gender-queer or other ambiguous forms of identification.

Narcissus and his myth are productively retold in images that, like Cahun's, refuse to believe in the fixity of identity and turn the perils of narcissism into a formative reflection on representation as shaping subjectivity. The next section deals with another perspective on portraiture, ostensibly the opposite of narcissism: portraiture in scientific photography. The focus here shifts from the self to the other. Through measurement, ways of lighting, and the making of visual comparisons, among other things, the third-person authority of medical-scientific discourse has bestowed particular kinds of identity on designated others.

FROM SCIENTIFIC DISPLAY TO ARTISTIC SELF-IMAGING

A prominent self-portrait by Del LaGrace Volcano (*Andro Del*, 2000; Fig. 6) shows some resemblance to Cahun's double portrait: it shows a bald-headed face, which, apart from the skin's obvious whiteness, appears to be free of identity markers such as age and gender.[16] The inexpressive close-up of the face, shot against what looks like a black-tile background, instantly reminds the viewer of laboratory photographs of criminals, queers, psychopaths, and other social outcasts, which became the basis for

---

16 As gender-variant visual artist Volcano rejects the use of gender specific personal pronouns and offers a first-person account of "myself." To write about Volcano's art from a third-person-perspective challenges the uses of gendered pronouns. I will attempt to do justice to this queering of gendered address by referring to Volcano's work by name or first person reference.

quasi-scientific theories about human normalcy and its corollary, deviance.[17] This particular self-portrait is taken from a series called *Gender Optional* (2000), in which Volcano portrays "my self" in ways which expose the impossibility of re/presenting intersex subjects.[18] They are a clear reference to the pathologization of subjects who were considered hermaphroditic and thus sexually deviant by the medical establishment. *Andro Del* specifically plays with the discrepancy between "exact science" (through measurement) and cultural indoctrination of bodily norms (through exemplifying the subject's aberrance against a normed framework). The intention of the artist is to *mark* these norms (like femaleness, maleness, whiteness) and to denaturalize them.[19]

---

17 The black and white background of the image is a card made to signify the "Lamprey system" of anthropometric photography for purposes of racial, sexual, and medical classification. The grid system was developed in the 1870s by John Lamprey, and was devised to make cross-racial comparison. See Maxwell: 29-47.

18 I want to stress that the series *Gender Optional* and much of the artist's oeuvre is dedicated and aesthetically invested in criticizing standard medical treatment of intersex subjects as it was historically and is currently practiced.

19 Volcano's artistic oeuvre includes photographs, installations, performance art and film. The artist's work complicates understandings of femininity and masculinity. The bodies in Volcano's works are described as "sites of mutation, loss, and longing." Notions of normal embodiment are queered in these photographs. Volcano states, "As a gender variant visual artist I access 'technologies of gender' in order to amplify rather than erase the hermaphroditic traces of my body. I name myself. A gender abolitionist. A part time gender terrorist. An intentional mutation and intersex by design (as opposed to diagnosis), in order to distinguish my journey from the thousands of intersex individuals who have had their 'ambiguous' bodies mutilated and disfigured in a misguided attempt at 'normalization.' I believe in crossing the line as many times as it takes to build a bridge we can all walk across" (http://www.dellagracevolcano.com, September 2005).

Fig. 6: Andro Del (Gender Optional)

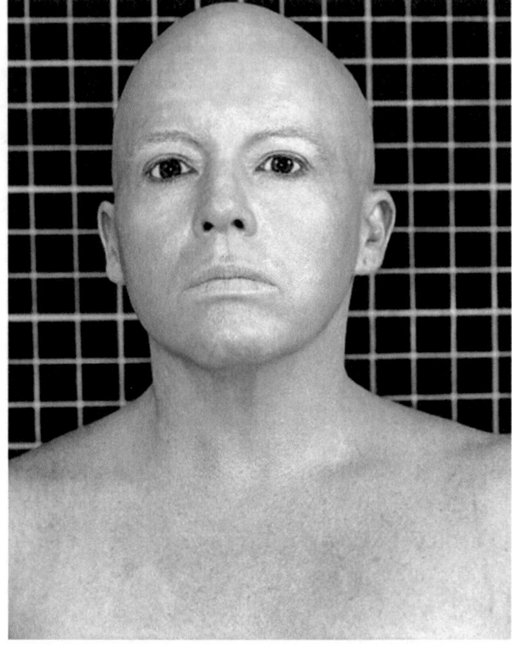

Source: Del LaGrace Volcano (2000)

Several images in *Gender Optional* consist of mug shots that show Volcano's face in differently aged and gendered stages against the same gridlike backdrop. The obviously staged character of Volcano's self-portraits does not entirely relieve the viewer from recalling criminological and psychiatric photographs, which have displayed their subjects as objectified types.

Andro Del, one of the starker face-shots in Volcano's image sequence, is revealing for the image's artificiality. The portrayed subject seems beyond humanity, lifeless and bloodless, as if sterilized by the laboratory practices of representation. The face is turned into an androgynous, indeterminate, desubjectivized mask. The skin is lit with blindingly bright light. As an effect, the black background grid breaks through the levels of the image, seeming to move toward the front, overwriting the face in the foreground. One cannot see the skin's wrinkles or creases. There is no hair visible, and the transitions between nose, mouth, eyes, ears, neck, and cheeks can barely be guessed. The one feature that stands out and cannot be securely located within the image, as they seem to hover between foreground and background, are the subject's eyes. They are dark blue, piercing, and cold.[20] In contrast to the rest of the photograph's black-and-white tonal scheme, the eyes are the only colored element, making them hard to place in the image. They take on a life of their own.

In his analysis of the work of contemporary transgender artists, Ben Singer shows how the subversive element in their images mainly lies in the subjects' look. Artists often picture themselves looking directly, almost provocatively, at the camera and the viewer. This use of the look corresponds to, and reverses, the import of the look in medical portraiture. The stare of the criminal or the mad person used to be singled out as dangerous and aggressive. Indeed, the fear of being seen by a degenerate led to a sense of personal vulnerability that was associated with the threat of violence (Fraser 1998: 145). The self-portraits of Volcano can be seen to cite and ridicule such pathological imaging.

Some transgender artists counter a laboratory-like atmosphere with chiaroscuro lighting, dark backgrounds, and self-assured posing as bodybuilders, fashion models, or businessmen. Probably the most famous transgender artist who posed as a nude bodybuilder is the photographer Loren Rex Cameron. In many of his self-portraits, he directly refers to the medical gaze by holding the shutter release bulb in one hand while his other hand injecting a syringe with body-modifying testosterone into his buttocks. Singer describes those images in the following way:

Cameron's [self-portraits refuse] the Frankensteinian logic of medical expertise that puts the doctor and the medical establishment in the role of the creator. ... While the medical model asserts that Cameron is a product of medical intervention – or even invention, and thus a proper subject of the medical gaze – [his self-images represent] him as an active moral and ethical agent assuming responsibility for his own embodiment. (Singer 2006: 606)

Despite their unquestionable significance for transgender emancipation, I have doubts about the critical potential of Cameron's photographs. They seem to subvert the traditional objectification of gender-queer subjects

---

20 The blueness of the eyes is a deliberate reference to Aryan ideals (personal email conversation with Volcano on 21 January 2014).

through their emphasis of Cameron's hypermasculinity. Posture, expression, and appearance in no way betray the artist's transgendered body—excepting perhaps the glimpse of the absent phallic bulge, slightly visible scars in place of breasts, and the syringe. The play with traditional masculinity is decisive, yet does not challenge representation's coercive mechanism.

In contrast to the representations of non-normative bodies that allude to trans-bodied beauty, muscles, and male stereotypes, Volcano subverts those same traditions in a different way. Like Cahun, Volcano strips gendered markers from his face. In doing so, the artist refers to the photographs of so-called sexual inverts that exhibited male and female features and whose sitters were difficult to identify. Lacking resemblance to conventionally gendered persons, these photographs possess an ambiguity that creates a void in the viewer's reading of the image. The depicted criminal, queer, or psychopath cannot be read through common signs of identity.

As Singer points out, since the nineteenth century scientific photographs have been used to document the moral depravity of criminals, homosexuals, and people with physical anomalies. Medicine, psychiatry, and criminology conspired to produce evidence of "a common aesthetic impulse: to locate the sight/site of deviance on the bodies of a wide array of social outcasts" (Singer 2006: 601). In line with social changes in the late nineteenth and early twentieth centuries, the medical sciences developed new strategies to deal with health problems, to cure illnesses, and to help maintain the sanity of individuals. The medical perspective developed from one characterized by learning about illnesses in books (library medicine) to the classification and management of a patient's symptoms (bedside medicine). With the advent of the first hospitals in Paris, the now dominant model of medicine in Europe and North America arose (hospital medicine).

This model's relation to visuality is of particular interest for this chapter. In his historical study of space, Michel Foucault focused on what John Rajchman (1988: 103) has characterized as "spaces of constructed visibility," such as hospitals and prisons. Foucault demonstrates how these spaces constitute the subject by determining her being in space through the monitoring of light, controlling what can be seen or not seen. As much as visual technologies were able to discipline bodies in "panoptic" architecture, surveillance medicine employed photography and portraiture in its efforts to "provide for" a population's health. The distancing from the body of the individual patient allowed for a new clinical picture. The increased focus on the space between bodies made it possible, on the one hand, to visually document health risks on a broader scale: the findings of surveys could be checked against a grid-like structure, in which individuals became readable through their differentiation from other subjects. This mapping of bodies created a picture of the containment of pathologies and an apparent totality. On the other hand, visual information, having become more important, also became more strongly relational. A clinical picture can mean something only in contrast to another of the same kind. This relationality was typically enacted in series of images about certain types of illness, embodiments, or criminal dispositions.

In "Queer Physiognomies" (2004), Dana Seitler shows how "racial peculiarities," "fetishism," "aberrations and perversions," and "freaks and other abnormalities" were illustrated in the scientific pictorial displays of the early twentieth century. The well-known headshot photographs of prisoners or sexual degenerates were often displayed in medical textbooks as a row of portraits, eliciting comparison. Not only did the pictured subjects inevitably refer to one another, but they also created a connection among a range of images showing bodies designated as deviant. Cahun's self-portrait alludes to those scientific headshots in its cold presentation of the two faces, stripped of attire or other markers of social origin or status. The duplication of the heads imitates images of Siamese twins, which were circulated under the aegis of showing anatomical abnormalities; moreover, the work mimics scientific comparisons between different purported degenerates. By letting the heads acknowledge their mutual assessment in the image, Cahun questions the impassivity or non-involvement of the subjects in their classification as a type. The externally determined relationality is transferred into the picture, allowing the portrayed to appropriate the act of comparison.

The development of what Kathryn Fraser terms the "photographic insane" (1998) became the basis for transgender artists to counter traditional, depersonalized medical representations with self-representative portraiture. Fraser observes how the use of portraiture and photography originally reinforced medical authority:

The use of codes of portraiture (e.g., images limited to representing the head and shoulders on a plain or non-existent background) and the choice to represent a posed subject rather than an arrested moment in time (such as a surgical procedure) all contributed to the increasing medicalization of such images. (144)

This practice had the additional effect of creating a visual model for the representation of a state of illness or insanity. To some extent, one could even say that the posed character of medical portraiture supported the objective aim to represent the deviation from a natural state of being.

This pathological relationality also incorporates the viewer of the images in a particular way. It exposes a visuality that refers to the other as part of a whole, a deviation from the normal, which at the same time has its place in the schema that map society. The viewer finds herself looking at a neighbor on a contingent categorical grid. This situation creates a viewing position that may provoke the spectator's apprehension about resembling or even becoming the clinical image.

Photographic portraiture was first practiced in the field of psychiatry in the early twentieth century. Its photographs did more than merely document knowledge about deviance; they also aimed to inform the public about codes of insanity and potential aberrations from racial and sexual norms.[21] A prevalent fear of cultural and moral contagion made the images an important marker to delineate the normal from the deviant, as Seitler observes:

Together, racial and sexual imagery in science's visual culture enabled the human sciences to delineate a framework of deviance – to affirm, through the degradation of a racialized, sexualized, and gender-troubled body, the virtues of social hygiene, and to protect, through the elevation of scientific certainty, the social world that so many feared was endangered by the presence of such deviant bodies. The imperative of visibility helped demarcate a formal space of legibility within which

---

21　See Bronfen 1992 on anxiety about portraits: "Anxiety about portraits expresses the fear that the transformation of matter from one form to another can engender the literal sacrifice of the 'depth' of the model. ... Anxiety is based on a confusion between the imaginary register with the real; a misunderstanding of the portrait as an iconic rather than an arbitrary symbolic sign; a misunderstanding that the production of an image can cause an incursion into the materiality of its object of reference. [It] reintroduces an uncertainty about the distinction between a body and its image" (115).

conceptualizations of human sexuality became available, but the compulsive and infinitely expanding nature of this imperative also fundamentally challenged sexuality as a stable or recuperable category. (80)

The fear of contagion and the imperative of visual exposition are contrary phenomena that are combined and exposed in Volcano's self-portrait. The portrayed face shows as much as can be shown of a face stripped of hair, shadow, and color; it is vulnerably naked. It exposes itself unambiguously to the eye of the viewer. The imperative of visibility is satisfied. At the same time, the stark blue eyes shoot a look at the viewer that seems to break through the picture plane, crossing the border separating sterile image and impure reality. The viewer is affected by the authority of the image and the control of the portrait's look. Volcano implements contagion within the image: the artist imports it into the self-representation, transforming moral panic into an actual effect of visual technology. The deviant's self-portrait becomes a confident performance of a social actor.

Jean-Luc Nancy argues that the portrait sets a subject within a relation to the self (2006: 227). His argument allows me to pose a crucial question regarding Volcano's self-portrait: How does the relation appear of the portrayed subject to its own self and to that of the spectator? What does it provoke? In "The Look of the Portrait" (2006), Nancy ascribes to the portrait a peculiar quality, namely a capability of looking (see also Didi-Huberman 1992). He claims that when the look of a subject is portrayed in a painting, the painting itself becomes the look it paints. The portrait's look, however, does not look at something, it merely embodies or accommodates a look that might at best look at nothing. The portrait presents a look that draws the viewer's eyes upon itself, that turns the spectator's look into its own reflection.

When Nancy discusses Miquel Barceló's *Double Portrait*, he observes the canvas's transmutation into a close-up of the look. The flat and skin-colored surface becomes the upper part of a face. The two black heads become eyes that stare lifelessly at the viewer. The look of Barceló's painting seems to disrupt a possible relation between the portrait and the spectator, as well as between the two portrayed faces. The viewer's sight is drawn into two black holes and devoured by the painting's eye-like look upon itself. In Volcano's self-portrait, however, the relation between the look *of* the image and the look *in* the image is more complicated. With its direct reference to medical portraiture's history of humiliating objectification, *Andro Del* incorporates the look of the portrait into Volcano's own look and returns it to the viewer. In contrast to Barceló, Volcano reproduces the portrait's look, and bestows it with a life of its own. The life of the portrait lies in the look. The face itself remains unresponsive, mirroring the deadening effects of visual objectification.

Volcano's spectral face reflects androgynous and lifeless, nearly inhuman or posthuman features, reminiscent of figures like androids, cyborgs, or humanoid aliens. Because of the skin's lack of contrast, caused by the photograph's bright lighting, the face drowns in its background. The effacement of detail turns into a *defacement*. Paul de Man has applied the notion of defacement to autobiographical writing (1979). He relates defacement to the production of new knowledge by stressing the act of writing on a surface, which lends the object a personified appearance. To deface is to infuse life onto a marred or dead object. De Man understands defacement as an effect of language that lends a face to something that does not have one; this new face can be understood as masking or naming something absent, deceased, or voiceless (926).

Transposing de Man's notion into the realm of the visual, I understand the "light-writing" of photography as a way to take a face's lifeless image and give it a new face. Cahun's photograph effaces any likeness to a human, living, gendered, and colored face. It defaces the representational truth of a photographic portrait. The face of Volcano is not, however, absorbed by nothingness, but presents instead an affective screen onto which new characteristics of humanity can be projected. It serves as a reflecting and reflected unity, which in its close-up appearance turns from reflexive to intensive. I am here following Deleuze's view of close-ups in films, which, as he suggests, do not represent a face, but *are* that face.[22] This effect, in addition to the use of white light intensifies the visual power of the close up, as Deleuze states:

[A translucent or white] space retains the power to reflect light, but it also gains anther power which is that of refracting, by diverting the rays which cross it. The

---

22 Deleuze argues that "there is no close-up of the face" but that "the close-up is the face" (1986: 88), and that the face's blankness or nudity represents an inhumanity that is "much greater than that of animals" (ibid: 99).

face which remains in this space thus reflects a part of the light, but refracts another part of it. From being reflexive, it becomes intensive. (1996: 94)

Similarly, Volcano's and Cahun's faces confront their viewer with an intensity that "forces the spectator to rebound on the surface of the screen" (ibid: 94). They thus present to the spectator a screen or façade, which overwrites the representational power of the portrait, and, as a consequence, the photographed subject's gendered, sexual, and racial characteristics. They show a particular nudity, which consists of skin stripped of common markers. Both images consequently convey a certain inhumanness, or a flatness of human expression, that could be compared to the characteristics of a phantom, defined by the Merriam-Webster Dictionary as "something (as a specter or an optical illusion) that is apparent to the sight or other sense but has no actual or substantial existence."

The ghostlike appearance of both images is produced through the effects of lighting. As in the medical portraits, Cahun and Volcano use bright white studio lighting. However, in contrast to the scientific aim to bring out as many visual details as possible, the two artists flatten or even erase the faces' features with this sort of light. Instead of absorbing and thus elucidating the illuminated faces, the artworks return the light, mirroring it in the white surfaces of Cahun's and Volcano's heads.

In a similar vein, Mieke Bal analyzes the ghostlike effect of lighting in portrait painting. In *Quoting Caravaggio* (1999), Bal suggests that light in painting takes on a particular material quality, like paint (189). Light and shade can form a tactile substance, produced by what Bal calls "light-writing." With this term, she refers to the art of "photo-graphy," which literally means "writing with light," and ascribes to it the ability to create a physical effect on the viewer. Bal writes: "Light signifies the most tender and slight, yet most thrilling, kind of touch" (ibid: 192). Engaging the viewer corporeally in the act of viewing, the light-written image makes itself available to a different kind of seeing. The color white, which in painting produces the impression of light, takes on a relevance beyond its material substance. It transcends the painting's surface, creates depth, permits an "inward" view of the image and of oneself. "White compels us to look closely. ... It is not a color because it is all colors: it reflects them," Bal concludes (ibid: 46-47).

Thus, white lighting also suggests a mirror function. Applied to photography, the material quality of white paint/pigment is replaced by the evanescent yet significant immateriality of projected lighting. Richard Dyer's essay on the relationship between whiteness and light in photography and film conclusively shows that both are used to produce certain aesthetic effects in vision. He emphasizes an obvious yet easily disregarded fact, namely that photographic images or frames of a projected film are products of the effect of light on a chemically prepared surface, a surface with light shining through onto a screen. Without light, there is no photograph and no film (Dyer 1997: 85). The elements involved in the production of a particular photographic image, such as the light source, the skin color of the depicted subject, or the exposure and development of the film material, all affect the way an image is perceived. Through these means, the image controls visibility and causes a particular touch for the viewer. Depending on the play of shadows, back- or front-lighting, and different tones of light, the surface of the image takes on mirrorlike qualities that can reflect a viewer's look or, alternately, act as a black hole that swallows the spectator's gaze. In photography, light becomes a medium of infinite plasticity (ibid: 84). It is textural yet evasive, evanescent yet invasive. In Volcano's and Cahun's photographs, the bright and cold studio lighting on white skin against a dark background creates an eerie feeling, a dizzying effect.

Another type of whiteness also plays an important role in the two images: the white paper on which the photographs are printed invades the images from across their borders and shows through the portrayed faces, blurring the difference between image or representation and outside reality. In the photographs, white covers as well as reveals most of the images' surfaces. The larger part of the images is white surface, giving the depicted figures a translucent, indistinct quality. Combined with the brutally sharp contours of the faces' outlines, which refer to the scrutinizing medical gaze in criminological, psychiatric, eugenic, and ethnographic photography, the images produce a dissonance between defined visibility and vague perception. What at first sight seems to present itself as a clear image turns out to create an opaque effect in the viewer. The sharp shapes against the background stand in contrast to the skin's undefined whiteness. The characteristic of whiteness lies in opacity rather than clarity. Gendered and racial details are effaced and become unrepresentable. A defined personality is likewise erased, and the erasure causes a ghostly presence to become evident. The very humanness of the portrayed faces is questioned.

The faces appear as faces; yet, they refute their subject's humanness. What both images expose, however, in clear contrast to Barceló's two heads, is an uncanny aliveness in their eyes and their sharp looks. It seems as if what they represent as subjects resides inside their heads, almost beyond visibility. The viewer is confronted with glimpses of a life that is projected outwards through their piercing gazes. The two-dimensional medium of the photographs becomes alive through the play of light and darkness reflected in the portrayed eyes. Cahun's and Volcano's images achieve this pictorial animation by unusual means: they give life to the visual image by effect of blinding their viewer. White and light effect blindness and nothingness in the viewer. All depth is lost in the white surfaces. The seemingly insubstantial black (or blue) parts of the images contain and give life to the represented subjects. Life exists within the image, almost behind the surface of the image, at the edge of visibility, and on the border of representation.

I submit that this effect is what makes up the *queering* aspect of the two images. They imitate a cultural tradition in such a way that it is turned on its head, enacted in reverse. Using the same means as artists within a venerable tradition, these artists subvert the usual outcome. They queer the visual by exposing what ought to remain concealed, and by disrupting the repressive surface of representational imaging. Butler defines queering "as a term for betraying what ought to remain concealed" (1993: 176). She states that "'queering' works as the exposure within language – an exposure that disrupts the repressive surface of language – of both sexuality and race" (ibid: 176). I want to use her conception of the term and apply it to the realm of the visual, where the disruption takes place on the surface of the picture by visual means and on the surface of representation by discursive means. Like Cahun's retelling of Narcissus's myth in *Que me veux-tu?*, the use of whiteness and the effects of light are changed in *Andro Del*. The images do more than merely rearticulate visual traditions; they enact new, queer, or disruptive ways of articulating or accounting for a self in and through visual means.

In light of this response to the history of portraiture, I would like now to explore the account these artists give of themselves through their images. What do these self-portraits reveal about the production of subjectivity in visual representation? The question of how a self becomes a self in a queer image is central. Coupled with the search for self is the *loss* of self, which has the potential to challenge the relation between subjectivity and visuality.

SHOWING AN ACCOUNT OF ONESELF

In the afterword to her book on the politics of mourning (2003), Judith Butler analyzes the productivity of loss when it becomes the condition for a new place in the world, a community, or one's body. For Butler, loss potentially constitutes new social, political, and aesthetic relations. In *Giving an Account of Oneself* (2005), Butler engages with the relationality of social recognition and the foreignness of language to the speaking and narrating self, which render the subject fundamentally "opaque to itself" (Butler 2001: 20). She argues that "recognition becomes the process by which I become other than what I was and so cease to be able to return to what I was. There is, then, a constitutive loss in the process of recognition, since the 'I' is transformed through the act of recognition" (ibid: 27-28). The loss of self, through the subject's opacity, may be constitutive of a new form of recognition: a recognition that is responsive to images of others, radical others as much as common social others. In this sense, subjectivity becomes fundamentally incomplete, dependent on the ethical space for divergent self-identifications. As Butler writes, "Sometimes the very unrecognizability of the others brings about a crisis in the norms that govern recognition" (ibid: 24). In line with Michel Foucault, she contends that "a certain risking of the self becomes the sign of virtue" (ibid: 24).

Subjectivity, in other words, depends on a form of dislocation. "The possibility of the 'I', of speaking and knowing the 'I'," Butler continues, "resides in a perspective that dislocates the first-person perspective whose very condition it supplies" (ibid: 23). This dislocation, which I perceive as a partial loss of self, is occasioned by the self's subjection to a set of cultural frames, or, in Foucauldian terms, by "the contemporary order of being," or, as Butler characterizes it, by the social structure of address. To know myself I must tell my story to someone, address someone. Address not only exposes myself to another, but also conditions my autobiographical account of myself. The "I" can only give an account of itself in relation to a "you." Or, as Butler observes: "without the 'you', my own story becomes impossible" (ibid: 24). Butler emphasizes the importance of mutual recognition as well as the irreducibility of the subject. "The uniqueness of the Other is exposed to me, but mine is also exposed to her, and this does not mean we are the same, but only that we are bound to one another by what differentiates us, namely, our singularity" (ibid: 25), she concludes.[23]

I want to stress three aspects of what it means to give an account of oneself in Butler's argument. First, such an account is never fully mine, nor is it ever fully for me, because it can only be given in addressing another. The form taken by this account depends on this other as much as on myself. Second, giving an account of myself happens under certain social and cultural conditions. Third, giving an account of myself produces narrative form. I tell my story *to you*. My story emerges in language, and because language comes before my own emergence, my account always arrives late. My account then is also partial, since there is a (bodily) history to my self, for which I can have no recollection. At the same time, I produce myself in narrative (re)construction and become accountable for who I am and what I do. This narrative construction of one's life, and the acknowledgement of the limits of self-knowledge in the face of the Other, according to Butler, ultimately form the basis for an ethical stance that desires to know who the other is without expecting to resolve this desire by getting a final answer. To keep alive the desire to know or the curiosity about others is crucial to the social practice of address, to mutual forms of recognition, and consequently to ethical responsibility. The question here may be: "What have I become in the face of you?"

In view of this interpretation, how do the self-portraits of Cahun and Volcano give a visual account of the subjects? I propose that Cahun and Volcano give an account of themselves by *visually* addressing others, and that they challenge the norms of recognition by addressing those others in specific ways. Visually accounting for a self might allow for a space of

---

23 Butler here uses Levinas's notion of the Other, which in contrast to Lacan's symbolic "Other" and to a specific "other," as other than myself, is a material, if not knowable or objectifiable, other person. The distinction is important because in Butler's argument the Other serves as a second-person Other, a "you," whom I encounter face to face and to whom I give an account of myself.

self-identification that lies outside common narrative structures: a space for ambiguous, norm-resisting, unsteady, or culturally lost selves.

In *Precarious Life* (2004), Butler is concerned with the potential failure of address and its precarious consequences for selfhood. Referring to Emmanuel Levinas's notion of the face, Butler links the social mechanisms of address to the conditions of representation:

When we consider the ordinary ways that we think about humanization and dehumanization, we find the assumption that those who gain representation, especially self-representation, have a better chance of being humanized, and those who have no chance to represent themselves run a greater risk of being treated as less than human, regarded as less than human, or indeed, not regarded at all. (141)

Humanity is often given or taken away by way of the face. Apparently, the face is not automatically always a *human* face in the contemporary order of representation. The deformed, extreme, or ambiguous face is not one to which we can easily relate. If the viewer cannot effectively connect to the represented face, she looks for identifiable markers beyond the portrait, outside the frame, and thus engages in a nonreciprocal relation with the represented face. But, these images ask, do images ever allow for a reciprocal relation between represented selves and their viewers?

I ask this question from the position of the pictured selves in Volcano's and Cahun's images. What might their questions to their others/viewers be? I want to suggest that Cahun asks: To whom do I give an account if there is no constitutive "you" to speak to, or if there is no "you" that recognizes me as a human subject? Cahun's practical answer is to reciprocally show (rather than narrate) herself to her other self, to a second self within or outside her. Cahun's face becomes a humanly recognized face in light of her own view of a split or doubled self. Akin to what Butler describes as an ethically significant incoherence or contingency of one's own story, Cahun presents to her viewer a representational impossibility – a double/split self – which exposes her own and the viewer's shared partial blindness about ourselves.

Butler's insights resonate with Cahun's attempt when she writes:

Although some would say that to be a split subject, or a subject whose access to itself is opaque and not self-grounding, is ... not to have the ground for agency and the conditions for accountability, it may be that this way in which we are, from the start, interrupted by alterity and not fully recoverable to ourselves, indicates the way in which we are, from the start, ethically implicated in the lives of others. (2001: 35)

Cahun's self-representation becomes a visual challenge to self-portrayal as the attempt to capture the truth about the represented self. It becomes an account of a self that anticipates the other, outside and within oneself, in the face of the other – Cahun's own face. Referring to Levinas, Butler says in this context: "The 'I' finds that, in the face of an Other, it is breaking down" (ibid: 36). I would add: In the face of oneself *as* Other, the "I" loses itself and gains access to a recognition that lies beyond the common norms of representation. The self here becomes more than "one self." It proffers an identity that is larger than a singular, defined self. This brings us back to Robin in *Nightwood*, who, calling to mind Lacan's mirror stage and the infant's self-alienation, "[knows] no desire because she coincides with herself" (van Alphen 1999: 157). Robin is seemingly free from alienation. She does not separate herself from her self to become a subject, but alienates others and turns into a non-subject, becoming unreadable as human. Since, as we saw, Robin is always addressed and never addresses others, the word "I" is of no use to her. As Matthew puts it: "She, the eternal momentary – Robin, who was always the second person singular" (Barnes 2001: 135). She is forever beyond the formation of an "I" and yet affects others with a particular force.

In Volcano's self-portrait *Andro Del*, the blue-eyed, steely look disturbs the reciprocity between the portrayed subject and the viewer. The motionlessness of Volcano's face, its slick surface without crease or wrinkle, and its agelessness and gender neutrality give the viewer few signs to identify (with). The look alone might invite a mutual exchange between spectator and portrayed, but although the sitter's eyes seem to look at *something*, they are not directed at a particular "you." Volcano's self-representation does not take up the position of an "I" that addresses a "you." Indeed, it does not seem to give an account of the portrayed subject at all. The blank look does not tell its observer anything about the presented subject. The eyes assert that there is nothing to say about the pictured self.

Here, the goal of self-presentation is not to tell the truth about the represented self. This is merely a self for itself, and thus, in reference to Butler's theory, a subject that defies exteriority and relations to others. *Andro Del* presents its viewer with a self that is shockingly absent from view, a self that does not represent itself to others but exists only in and through itself. We see a subject that is utterly narcissistic, and possibly exhibitionistic, yet completely unrevealing to others. In this kind of self-presentational narcissism, it seems, the self loses itself in representation and exists only beyond the frame of the image. By disavowing the position of first-personhood, the subject disorients the viewer's position as a "you" and thus complicates the relation between self and other, so that neither can successfully give an account of themselves.

With such questioning of the tradition of portraiture, Cahun and Volcano explore their selves' visual presence or absence through and in self-portraits. Cahun severs the representational ties between the sitter and the image's content. Volcano amasses and merges so many references – the countless anonymous faces of medical photography – that the link to an individual sitter becomes impossible. Cahun's and Volcano's photographs advocate an attempt to *overcome* subjectivity.

Cahun's and Volcano's self-portraits perform almost self-less forms of selfhood that are contingent on the absence of identity and representational markers. They show forms of selves that are visible only beyond or outside of the representational codes of portraiture.

4 Absence in Mapplethorpe's Wake

> The photographer's look is looking in a pure state; in looking at me, it desires what I am not – my image.
>
> SUSAN SONTAG

> Seeing death in blackface requires an impossible identification – seeing black *is* being black when black bodies perform in the space of death.
>
> SHARON PATRICIA HOLLAND

> It is not about what the subject is, but about how the subject is seen.
>
> ROBERT MAPPLETHORPE

The auditorium is illuminated but the stage is blacked out, and the murmurs, laughter, and whispers of the incoming audience are disrupted by a metallic-sounding "click–click–click." The imitated sound of a camera shutter, irregularly repeated, amplified by the theatre's loudspeakers, and spreading as if it were coming from above and from behind the audience, serves as the opening of a tribute to artist Robert Mapplethorpe (1946-1989) by the contemporary African-Brazilian dancer Ismael Ivo (b. 1955). In Ivo's *Mapplethorpe* (2002), as the audience files into the auditorium, this sound envelops them, so as to make them want to turn around and discover who is watching and taking pictures. The repeated clicking momentarily exposes the power inherent in the sound of taking a photograph. It discloses the theatre spectator's visibility and vulnerability vis-à-vis an outside viewer – someone behind a camera, unseen. Simultaneously spectator and part of the spectacle, the audience of *Mapplethorpe* is confronted with the reciprocal mechanisms of visuality.[1]

This scene takes place before the dance performance starts. This is significant because the spectator is unaware that she is being watched. The soundscape provided by the repeated action of camera shutter creates a double state of spectatorship. It makes the audience aware of their own noise, the sounds they make while talking to friends, or coughing, or scraping the floor with their shoes; it is as if the unexpected clicking creates a auditory screen against which other, largely unconscious sounds can be perceived. The perception of one's own stirring, and consequently of one's physical presence in space, creates a new awareness of the space from which one looks at the stage. The auditorium becomes an area that will, for the duration of the show, be dark and mostly invisible, but at first it registers something unrepresented yet significant: the seeming absence of the spectators.

In addition, the sound of the camera shutter also establishes a connection to the visual sense. This modest noise represents one of the most revolutionary means of viewing the world. The photographic practice of observing and capturing the world from the position of being behind a technical device – in early photography, behind a black veil – is here abstracted in the sound of a click, which evokes for the viewer the confusion between the presence of the other as photographer and her own viewing position. The exterior and interior spaces of the theatre hall overlap, and the viewer finds herself watched, possibly photographed.

In her analysis of the significance of sound and voice in cinema (*The Acoustic Mirror*, 1988), Kaja Silverman casts the *photo session* as a symbolical fulfillment of the function of constituting subjectivity and manifesting the look of the other through a "click." By discussing Luce Irigaray's concept of desire and Jacques Lacan's definition of the gaze,

---

1 *Mapplethorpe* had its premiere at the Biennale di Venezia in 2002. Choreography and dance: Ismael Ivo; light design and sound: Heinze Baumann; set design and costumes: Marcel Kaskeline; music: Steve Reich, Giacomo Puccini. The dance performance was created for the opening of the dance biennale "SoloMen" in Venice, 2002 (director: Carolyn Carlson).

Silverman identifies "two crucial ways of understanding the subject's relation to visual representation, both of which stress his or her captation – the mirror stage and the 'photo-session'. In the former, he or she incorporates an image, and in the latter, he or she is appropriated as image" (Silverman 1988a: 161). Lacan theorizes the order of the "imaginary" as a state in every subject's life that functions as an internalized image of the subject's ideal and coherent self, which is not yet alienated from itself. The mirror stage thus concerns the imaginary; the photo session, in contrast, relates to the symbolic, through which the subject starts to relate to others.[2] Silverman writes:

The pictorial metaphor through which [the] heightened sense of self is communicated to us is startlingly close to the image through which Jacques Lacan's *The Four Fundamental Concepts of Psycho-Analysis* "visualizes" subjectivity, adding as it does the notion of what I have … called "the photo session" to that of the mirror stage as "formative of the I". Significantly, this exaggerated self-awareness coincides with the primal scene. … Subjectivity is thus put in place … through the pictorial (or as Lacan would have it, the photographic) surface, rather than through the projection of psychological depth. It is the consequence of a *mise-en-scène* – of the deployment of bodies within a spatial logic – and of the play of the gaze across that *mise-en-scène*. (Silverman 1988b: 155-56)

Photography exaggerates one's self-awareness, because it marks being seen by an other. The camera, Silverman contends, is a signifier for the gaze that is outside. And according to Jacques Lacan, this gaze determines a subject at the most profound level in the field of vision.[3]

---

2   For more on Lacan's theory of the mirror stage, see Lacan 2006. For more on Silverman's concept of the photo session, see Silverman 1988a: 161-62.

3   In a critical and race-sensitive reading of Lacan's theory of subject formation in the mirror stage, Shannon Winnubst (2004) contends that Lacan's thesis is necessarily based on ocularcentric sensibilities that dominate our contemporary culture. The reliance on sight, images, and visual reflections, she argues, is connected to a disavowal of race and racism. In Winnubst's view, Lacan's discourse implies a universal structure, which, although not entirely ahistorical, draws on ideological sources that enact a racism, which is endemic to our cultural landscape (29).

Ivo's performance illustrates Silverman's ideas and moves beyond them by transforming the seemingly safe and anonymous space of the auditorium into a vulnerable site, laying bare every spectator's participation in the spectacle they are about to consume. The conventions of theatrical space, and the boundaries within it, are shattered by a click. Ivo's audience experiences the potential loss as well as the affirmation of their identity as spectators when they are confronted with the click before they actually see anything on stage. The sound discloses the presence of another spectator, gazing at the viewers in the dark and hailing them into a situation of seeing and being seen.

At one point during *Mapplethorpe*, Ivo positions himself, naked, on a metal ramp that recalls a fashion-show catwalk as well as a bench for animal slaughter. Again we hear the insistent and by now irritating sound of a camera shutter, accompanied by the almost painfully attenuated mechanical reverberation of the camera's winder. Everything is dark except for the lighting of Ivo's legs and lower torso; with every click of the imaginary camera, the light cuts his body into distinct white squares, as if he were being dissected into singular, detached limbs. The dark skin radiates the projected light and takes on an amorphous color, shining, nearly lifeless. Exposed to what appears to be the camera's humiliating gaze, Ivo addresses the sound with timid and resistant movements. His face is invisible, and thus his seeming distress can only be gleaned from his inhibited motion. But, occasionally, merely for seconds, the subject of this photo session, legs spread widely, seems in some way to respond to an erotic tension created by the simultaneous anonymity and intimacy of the scene.

In these instances, the viewer's position becomes problematic in her complicit desire for a body that is at once beautiful and racialized. Now it seems as though the spectators are allied with those who look through the camera's lens: they appear to be pressing the button, arranging the light, determining the set-up, situating themselves outside of the image they see. The audience's role shifts from passive observation to involvement in such a way that they seem to release the shutter and determine which part of Ivo's body is seen. They seem, in short, to choreograph the scene. By visually fragmenting Ivo's body, eventually they come to desire what Ivo is not – his image, split and distorted by a collective look.

Linking the spectator's desire for the image to the practice of photography, Geoffrey Batchen, in *Burning With Desire: The Conception of Photography* (1999), writes that "photographs are always catalysts for, and foci of, that desire invested in looking" (10-11). Following Batchen, I want to suggest that the object of this desire is only a trace, a transient flicker of light in one's inner eye. The real object on stage, Ivo's body, is irretrievably absent. In *Mapplethorpe*, Ivo thematizes the problematic of those bodies that have been underrepresented yet at the same time visually exploited (e.g., in colonialist and ethnographic studies of racially othered persons): bodies that have been *overlooked*.

In *The Absent Body*, Drew Leder observes that absence is linked to being:

The word *absence* comes from the Latin *esse*, or "being," and *ab*, meaning "away." An absence is the being-away of something. The lived body, as ecstatic in nature, is that which is away from itself. Yet this absence is not equivalent to a simple void, a mere lack of being. The notion of being is after all present in the very word *absence*. The body could not be away, stand outside, unless it had a being and stance to being with. (22)

Through its relation to being, absence is linked to the living body on the one hand. On the other, absence relates to a structural negativity. *Ab-esse* is being away, not being here, being dead – or, within a photograph, having-been-there, as Roland Barthes affirmed (1977: 4). Absence is where the living body and its potential negativity meet.

In this chapter, I want to analyze the potential of absence for the representation of bodies that have not been overlooked but, rather, have been "looked over" within the realm of a particular, discriminatory, and/or neglectful visual practice; a practice that has been formed by an economy of visibility, an aesthetic economy with political consequences for the construction of the image of the other. The other is fixed in and through the image that participates in a cultural fantasy that is often racist and sexist. I make use of the concept of absence as a tool to analyze the link between bodies and their absences, which is to say their images. If viewers are confronted with the negative aspect of visual presence in art, they become aware of the constructed relation between living bodies and their representations. In my view, the idea of absence disrupts the seeming coherence of this relation, and helps to develop alternative ways of imaging or imagining those bodies that have been subjected to representational stereotyping and pictorial neglect.

In particular, I am interested in the productive quality of absence in photography and (dance) performance. My objects of analysis in the present chapter engage with the art of Robert Mapplethorpe. In his work, we see how the notion of absence is inherent to both photography and performance. At this point, I would like to make a distinction between notions of absence as having-been-there – which is, following Barthes, crucial to photography – and as disappearance (or what I would like to call presence-as-absence), which is, I claim, essential to performance art when it is defined as representation without reproduction.

My argument follows three lines of thought. First, I explore photography's historical relation to the concept of death. From its very beginnings photography has been occupied with arresting moments in the lives of human beings so as to conserve them for future generations. The bond between photography and death has thus been strongly linked to the experience of absence and loss. Second, I address the idea of excess in representation. If something is absent from an image, it is either invisible or unrepresentable. Both instances motivate us to think about the place of this pictorial absence: Is it in our perception or in the image? In my exploration of this place, the notion of excess offers the possibility to look beyond, behind, and beneath the layers of the image. There is always more to representation than we can see. My third line of thought deals with the process of becoming-image. I argue that bodies can only be pictured by being exposed to the risk of partly losing their subjectivity. Becoming an image, then, means disappearing from oneself in the realm of representation. Throughout my analysis, a prominent role is given to stereotyped, neglected, overrepresented, unmarked, racialized, and sexualized bodies.

PHOTOGRAPHY IN THE FACE OF DEATH

The essential link between photography and death finds an instance as early as 1840. The works of Hippolyte Bayard (1801–1887), among the first photographs, provide three variations of the photographer depicted as a dead man in *Le Noyé – Self-portrait as a Drowned Man*.[4] As Geoffrey Batchen explains, this picture refers to other images by the same photographer, in which he presents himself, not unlike the vases, straw hats, and porcelain figurines that surround him, as an object among the world of things. Bayard stages a mock suicide as if he were speaking from beyond the grave to future beholders. On the back of one of the three prints of *Le Noyé* is a purported (though obviously untrue) suicide note, bitterly playful, in which he explains how "the Government, which has supported M. Daguerre more than is necessary, declared itself unable to do anything for M. Bayard and the unhappy man threw himself into the water in despair" (Batchen 1999: 167-71).

In his note, Bayard also makes the beholder believe that the discolored, darkened patches of skin in the image have resulted from the advanced decomposition of his corpse: "Ladies and Gentlemen, you'd better pass along for fear of offending your sense of smell, for as you can observe, the face and hands of the gentleman are beginning to decay" (ibid: 171). Stressing not only the visual but also the odorous dimension of the encounter with his corpse's image, Bayard animates the photograph from within the image. In other words, Bayard's image comes alive through the staging of his supposedly dead body as particularly uncanny. Its representation of death is what gives the photograph its special vivacity.

Here, the subject of death is linked to the process of photography. As the print of the photograph passes through time, being handled years after its creation, the "corpse" in the image seems to decompose further and eventually to dissolve the representation of the body. The photograph then becomes an allegory for what Belting, in "Image, Medium, Body: A New Approach to Iconology" (2005), describes as the absence of the body in the image. In his theory of embodied iconology, Belting links the remembrance of the dead to the medium of the image, which, by picturing the missing (now dead) body, allows for a "'symbolic exchange' between a dead body and a live image" (307). Belting states: "The image of the dead, in the place of the missing body, the artificial body of the image (the medium), and the looking body of the living [interact] in creating iconic presence as against

---

4   The three images are reproduced and extensively analyzed in Batchen 1999. They all are dated 18 October 1840 (direct positive print; Société Française de Photographie, Paris).

bodily presence" (ibid: 307). The iconic presence of the dead thus replaces bodily presence and renders the body absent in the image. Is this absence of physical presence in the image particular to images of the dead? Or, thinking with Barthes, is it not the case that (photographic) images are produced through and beyond the lethal effect of taking a picture, by refuting, in the moment of the click, the aliveness of the imaged subject.

As Belting shows elsewhere (2000), the absence of the human body in the image is a historical consequence of our culture's creation of the *Bildkörper*, the body of/in the image. The *Bildkörper* is a constructed representation of the mortal body, which cannot survive its iconicity. The human body is transformed, grows older, falls ill, recovers, and eventually dies; yet, it becomes another body in the image, the *Bildkörper*. Belting partly ascribes this effect to the idealization of the human body, which, in its model form, no longer belongs to a human being, shedding its capacity to stay alive in its iconic representation. Losing the body to the image is heightened through the technology of photography, in which the sitter's pose, as Barthes observes, becomes an image of its own even before the photograph itself materializes in the development process; a process that, with the advent of digital photography, has become almost instantaneous, yet has not lost its significance. The medium, which allows infinite copies to be made from a single negative or a single pose, also makes it possible to produce several different images of the same person without, however, coming closer to this person's actual look.[5] Again, the body's image, in a multiplied form, replaces the body's realness. Whose body do we see in an image of a body? And: who creates this body-image, if not the body itself?

The issue of the referential body's relation to its authorial power similarly surfaces in Bayard's image. The authorial power, commonly attributed to the photographer behind the camera, is doubted and ultimately negated. On the one hand, the calculated confusion about when and by whom the photograph has been made leads to uncertainty about the position or intention of the person behind the camera. How can a dead subject have pictured himself in a photograph? How, if the depicted dead body is the author's, can he have written the accompanying lines after the picture was developed? Even though the ruse might be obvious to an attentive viewer,

---

5   Below I discuss the still image's relation to motion. The "real" person I refer to here is the person, or body, in motion.

it creates an uncanny sensation; by obscuring the means of the image's production, the photograph suggests the death of the photographer as author. The image's object (a dead body) turns into the image's condition of creation (a dead author).

Taking my analysis further, I want to follow two threads that emerge from Bayard's *Le Noyé*. The first is the link between the image, what can be seen in the photograph, and what lies beyond its frame. I am interested in the absent but embodied presence in an image. This can either be the diseased authorial figure of the image or the viewer's gaze, which embodies an unseen presence within the texture of the photograph. Photography's quality may expose what Laura E. Tanner calls "the ever present gap between the living-moving body and the body as image" (2006: 14). Secondly, I will look at the asynchronism in the emergence of the image, which is perceived as a form of absence.

During the viewer's experience of Ivo's danced *Mapplethorpe*, the split between image and body becomes tangible. Ivo's second act performs a mirror scene. At the back of the theatre space, a set of two-meter-high mirror panes runs across the starkly illuminated stage. The white floor in front of the mirror wall is reflected in the blending glass. Naked, Ivo lies facing the mirror and slowly rolls his body into the white light. His dark skin stands in stark contrast to the whiteness of the scene. Accompanied by loud percussion sounds, his motions are interspersed with faraway human shouts and calls. Exposed to the light, Ivo seems agonized by what he glimpses from his mirror-image at the moments he faces it. When the dark body progresses from one side of the floor to the other, the audience gets to see a fractured mirror-image of that body. What had appeared to be a seamless mirror turns out to contain cracks and splits where different panes meet.

Ivo's mirror-image brings these irregularities to the fore. Consequently, the dancer's body looks fragmented, not so much by the cracks in the mirror but by the mirror itself. In other words, while the mirror itself looks continuous and whole, the image it produces of Ivo's body is jagged and slightly contorted. The smooth (white) mirror seems to generate an uneven image of the dancer's (dark) body. After a short blackout, during which the music gets louder, Ivo is again exposed to the same hard light, but he is now wearing a long-sleeved white shirt. The scene repeats itself until, after another short blackout, the dancer appears wearing long white pants to complement the shirt. By now, Ivo's black skin is nearly completely hidden; the viewer can barely see a body at all, and is confronted with a blank space on stage, where Ivo's body is represented merely by a face, hands, and feet.

When the music abruptly stops toward the end of the scene, the moving body slows down. Ivo carefully examines himself in the mirror. The mirror scene's conclusion suggests a certain curiosity toward the white image of the black body. But the scene as a whole communicates the blankness and bleakness conveyed by the white light, which over-visualizes the black body, filling the space's void for its audience while simultaneously fragmenting it for the mirrored black subject.[6] What becomes visible is the gap between the body and its image. Ivo shows that the image depends on the body that is imaged as well as the light in which it is represented. In exposing the split between his mirror-image (self-image) and the spectator's view of his body, Ivo reflects on a representational loss of substance, or an absence of particularly gendered, racial, and cultural bodies in the viewer's construction of images.

Another kind of absence related to *Mapplethorpe*'s enactment of the gap is also reflected in Bayard's *Le Noyé*: the lack of concurrence in time. The viewer of the image is confronted, at any point in time, with the asynchrony of events that led to the production of the image. Bayard's supposed death must have occurred before the shot was taken, or else he could not have been photographed as a dead man. At the same time, Bayard must have been alive to make the picture of himself; *Le Noyé* is a self-portrait. During the irreproducible leap in time between the making and the

---

6   In *Mapplethorpe: Polaroids* (2007), Sylvia Wolf observes Mapplethorpe's tendency to explore the self in his photographs, often with the help of mirrors or windows, as fragmented and multiple. Ivo's mirror scene speaks to this feature of Mapplethorpe's art and responds to a tradition among African American artists (including Richard Bruce Nugent and Richmond Barthé) of mediating a conflicted sense of self through their art. James Smalls describes this trend in *The Homoerotic Photography of Carl Van Vechten*: "It is the condition of the black subject to be splintered into multiple fragments of identity, to be identified from without within the confines of the modern experience that becomes the basis for the formation and the deformation of identity in the act of image-making" (2006: 122).

viewing of the image, Bayard's skin appears to have decayed and to have left a stain that will linger in the beholder's imagination of the depicted body.

In similar ways, Barthes, in *Image, Music, Text* (1977), explains the particular relation of the photograph to the passing of time when he writes that the spirit of the photograph lies in its showing of what has been there, or what is not there anymore:

The type of consciousness the photograph involves is indeed truly unprecedented, since it establishes not a consciousness of the being-there of the thing ... but an awareness of its having-been-there. What we have is a new space-time category: spatial immediacy and temporal anteriority, the photograph being an illogical conjunction between the here-now and the there-then. (44)

This relationship between the aliveness of a photograph and the enactment of death, as well as the representation of absence in the photographic image of a body, bears on my combined analysis of Mapplethorpe's photograph and Ivo's dance performance in the next section.

POLITICS OF ABSENCE

In her influential book on performance theory, *Unmarked: The Politics of Performance* (1993), Peggy Phelan conceptualizes a politics of absence. She attempts "to find a theory of value for that which is not 'really' there, that which cannot be surveyed within the boundaries of the putative real" (1). However, Phelan does not, as do various forms of minoritarian identity politics, call for greater visibility for the hitherto unseen. Instead, she questions the politics involved in the coercive powers of representational logic. The unmarked, for Phelan, marks the limits of the image for the racial and sexual other. Her resistance to visibility is motivated by the risk of securing specific images of that other, which thus restrains her from creating alternative forms of subjectivity. In the contemporary politics of the visual exposure of the self and the other – as in surveillance practices at political borders and the collapse of privacy in the public sphere – the alleged real and the representational are easily confounded. The assumption that what can be represented must necessarily be true fails to recognize the complex relation between reality and image.

The danger of visibility lies in its merely repeating the once-formed image of the conceptual cultural other to accommodate current hegemonic ideology and to eliminate deviation. In reference to culturally less-represented and politically disregarded social groups, Phelan says that "[in] framing more and more images of the hitherto under- represented other, contemporary culture finds a way to name, and thus to arrest and fix, the image of that other" (ibid: 2).[7] To counter this effect, Phelan's aim is to find what is unmarked in and absent from the image, or what is in excess of what we can see. In her eyes, excess resists representation and generates possibilities for what has been, until now, the unmarked or non-visible aspects of a subject.

Following Lacan, Phelan asserts the constituting role of the external gaze: "In looking at the other the subject seeks to see itself" (ibid: 16). She goes on: "Seeing the other is a social form of self-reproduction. For in looking at/for the other, we seek to re-present ourselves to ourselves" (ibid: 21). The image of the other simultaneously serves as a screen that reflects as well as obscures the *moi*. Self and other become dependent on each other for imag(in)ing identity. The process of becoming-subject, then, involves a seeing of oneself being seen by the other (Silverman 1992: 127). Phelan, however, warns of the risk of a complete substitution of self-image for the image of the other, which is always formed within the aesthetic economy of the white male gaze. One cannot and should not aspire to become the image of an other.

Phelan instead calls for fostering a still impotent (because unpracticed) inward gaze that produces self-seeing, a condition that exposes the subject to a potential blindness, the inability to see the non-visible: "[Until] one can accept one's internal other as lost, invisible, an unmarked blank to oneself and within the world, the external other will always bear the marks and scars of the looker's deadening gaze" (Phelan 1993: 26). The seeing of

---

7   Phelan does not define her use of "other" specifically, but she generally applies
     it to either the psychoanalytic notion of the other versus the self or to women
     and racial as well as ethnic minorities – groups of people who do not determine
     the hegemonic order of visual representation but who are often subjected to the
     coercion of an ideologizing visibility politics.

oneself fails to produce a complete picture of oneself. It is dependent on the look of the other's seeing, creating a blind spot where the other's self will be reflected in one's self-image. To see oneself is to be within the spectacle, which leaves a blank where seeing collides with being seen. For Phelan, this blank space resides outside the visible and thus outside representation. Yet, this absence can be productive and may have a binding relationship to the visible. Both aspects are expressed in the notion of the "after-image," the shadow of an image that remains in one's mind as a memory of the perceived, a trace of the visible. It is itself invisible, yet constitutes the visible in retrospect, and possibly in prospect. I demonstrate below that Mapplethorpe's *Self-Portrait* from 1985 plays on this idea of the after-image. It makes visible what Phelan attributes to the realm of the invisible. And it explores the possibility, and potential failure, of self-seeing.

In Mapplethorpe's *Self-Portrait,* we see his own gaze revealed to the spectator. Mapplethorpe examines his look, which has so often been criticized for objectifying and othering his African-American models. Next to Mapplethorpe's flower still lifes, his photographs of nude black men are probably his most famous photographs. Because they seem as aesthetically pure or clean as his flower photographs, Mapplethorpe's black nudes are vulnerable to that accusation. While they seem to fix the black body through the immobile, statue-like quality of the figures, most of them are also excessively sexual, showing erect penises and erotically suggestive postures. *Man in Polyester Suit* (1980) is perhaps one of the most extreme of the photographs that have been flagged to accuse Mapplethorpe of displaying a racially insensitive – or racist – attitude. It shows a man in a cheap polyester suit, whose half-erect penis is prominently exposed because his fly is unzipped. The man's head is cropped and his well-manicured, elegant hands are held slightly forward at his sides, in an expectant posture. Apart from the hands, only the penis identifies the model as a black man. Although this composition can be cited as a problematic example, the image remains ambivalent to the racist nature of the representation.

In his article "Looking for Trouble" (1991), Kobena Mercer defends Mapplethorpe's textual and sexual ambivalence in this and other images: "[the] shock of recognition of the unconscious sex-race fantasies is experienced precisely as an emotional disturbance which troubles the spectator's secure sense of identity" (189). Mercer argues that racist vision lies not within the image but in the viewer's fantasmatic and visual projection. *Man in Polyester Suit* may throw the viewer's potentially racist view back to her, and brings it to the fore as a problematic, if perhaps unconscious, way of looking that is part of prevailing ways of seeing bodies. In a similar way, I claim, Mapplethorpe throws his own gaze back upon himself in his 1985 *Self-Portrait* (Fig. 7).

Fig. 7: Self-Portrait

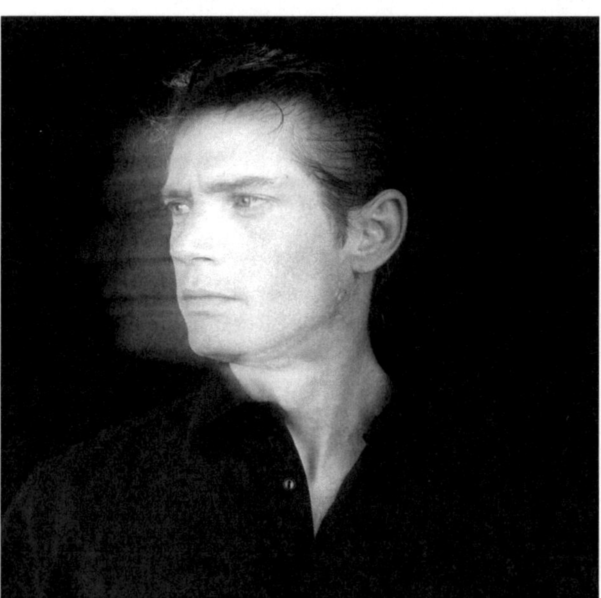

Source: Robert Mapplethorpe (1985), © Robert Mapplethorpe Foundation

Mapplethorpe's *Self-Portrait* from 1985 shows his stern face looking blankly at something beyond the frame. His face and neck are brightly illuminated; his eyes are cold, with a silvery sheen to them. The rest of the image is black, with almost no contours but an indication of the light that shines on his right shoulder, a hint of light that comes from far away, to where his look is drawn. The only anomaly in the otherwise classic posture is a transparent white smear that renders in a distorted blur his face's outline against the black background of the image.

This negative lucent shadow, an inverted shade, is suspended in a moment of arrested time. It seems to represent the fleetingness of vision, allowing for a glimpse of an illuminated presence, momentarily caught on film. But it portends disappearance. Is it one of Mapplethorpe's allegories of death, in this case, his own?[8] Or is it a glimpse of his self as a negative image, one that can be seen only as an ephemeral impression, hovering between two moments in time? Does Mapplethorpe here visually invoke what Phelan calls his internal other?[9] If so, Mapplethorpe takes the experiment of self-seeing a step further: he makes the image of his self-viewing visible to others. He thus reverses his role as photographer and makes his distorted vision of himself accessible to another's look. The role-reversal is repeated and intensified by the inversion of colors: the typically black body set against a white screen here becomes a white face within a black image. Thus, Mapplethorpe stages his self-portrait as a *negative*.

Phelan has discussed Mapplethorpe's tendency toward a form of self-portraiture that is characterized by forms of disguise. The self-portraits suggest a persistent negation of the possibility of capturing the self in a photographic image. Phelan writes: "Mapplethorpe's [...] self-portraits arrest the self-image as it slides into becoming an image of an 'other.' The image captured by the camera is an image which is performed in order to define the central absence of the self-image" (1993: 40). By calling into question the self-representation in his photographs of himself, Mapplethorpe frames the habitually unmarked white gaze within the image, which symbolizes, in his case, the absence of the black body from the white man's gaze, or the deficiency inherent in the photographer's gaze when picturing black bodies. The artist's ability to mark within the photograph

---

8   In 1986, only a year after taking this photograph, Mapplethorpe was diagnosed as HIV-positive. He then began to photograph himself with skulls and other symbols relating to death, inspired mostly by his fascination with Catholicism. Mapplethorpe died from an HIV-related infection in 1989.

9   In his early Polaroid photographs, Mapplethorpe expresses a recurring concern with the multiple facets of the self. See Wolf 2007: 22. The fragmented or distorted self might be compared to the notion of an internal other, a part of the self that is unfathomable, almost lost to one's grasp.

the unmarked – time, whiteness, the self – suggests Phelan's reflections on vision. The technique of extended exposure has created a ghostly second face. Again, the self-portrait allows for an analogy with Bayard's *Le Noyé*: they both leave behind a visible trace of the passing of time, something that in other circumstances would be invisible. Both images display a mark (stained skin/streak of light) caused by different photographic means. The skin on Bayard's hands and face looks stained because of its earlier exposure to sunlight. In the photographer's direct positive process of developing the image, the reddened parts turn black. Batchen even suggests that Bayard uses this photographic effect to draw attention to its "trickery as a mere illusion of the real, as well as to the artifice of the actual text and image we are seeing" (1999: 171). Bayard as well as Mapplethorpe thus perform absence as presence: the presence of something invisible in the image.

Such visual performances seem to undermine Phelan's emphasis on performance's productivity through its letting-go of the visible:

Performance's only life is in the present. Performance cannot be saved, recorded, documented, or otherwise participate in the circulation of representations *of* representations: once it does so, it becomes something other than performance. To the degree that performance attempts to enter the economy of reproduction it betrays and lessens the promise of its own ontology. Performance's being, like the ontology of subjectivity proposed here, becomes itself through disappearance. (Phelan 1993: 146; emphasis in original)

The unmarked in Phelan's theory shows itself through the negative and through disappearance. Disappearance is an active vanishing, a refusal to be lured into visibility. An example of this kind of productive disappearance is the work of the Guerrilla Girls, a group of women artists and feminist activists based in New York. They exhibit their political art in public places without revealing their identities. By wearing gorilla masks during their interventions, they refuse to participate in the currency of visibility. Disappearance, in relation to absence, is thus constituted by an act or by a conscious movement into nonappearance, while absence can be defined through its lack of coming or moving into visibility, a form of passivity. However, both notions relate to something missing or to the state of not-being-there, a not-being-there (anymore) in consciousness or in visuality.

Disappearance and absence can be used according to the respective realms in which one seeks to explain the cause of a blank, a negative, an impossibility, an ambivalence, or something missing. Phelan links the effect of disappearance in performance to the passing of time, as do Bayard and Mapplethorpe, albeit in different ways. In seeming contrast to Phelan's conception of performance, under which she also to some extent groups photography, Mapplethorpe's and Bayard's self-portraits aim to perpetuate or freeze the disappearing elements of artistic performance, which help the fleeting arts in reproducing the hegemonic ideology. Does this mean that Mapplethorpe and Bayard, in perhaps different ways, defy the critical potential of their art?

Ivo's dance also seems to reverse performance's power of disappearance through its references to Mapplethorpe's well-known images. Furthermore, the reference to photography as a visual medium brings up every image's unavoidable relation to reproducible technology or persistent iconology. I want to suggest here that precisely the seizing of performance's fleetingness, the halting and exposure of the image's construction of the body, makes us aware of the real body's absence in images. What Phelan means by the excess of representation is something that she positions beyond the image. I focus on the excess of representation *within* images of the body. That excess, rarely or barely visible to the naked eye, both Ivo and Mapplethorpe seek to perform as a crack in the image, a loss of the self (Mapplethorpe) or a failure to represent a subjective, whole body (Ivo) in a culture that is dominated by the white, male, straight, gaze.

PRODUCTIVE VISION

In *The Threshold of the Visible World* (1996), Kaja Silverman discusses a different kind of excess. With reference to Lacan's description of the subject's relation to the image, which she illustrates through the phenomenon of mimicry, Silverman gives particular weight to the concept of the stain. Silverman explains how a subject assumes "the shape of either a desired representation or one that has come through less happy circumstances to mark the physical body" (201). The stain is a form, a color, or a shape we wear to approximate a particular image before we become that image. Silverman suggests that thinking the subject's relation to the image through the metaphor of the stain allows for a better understanding of this relation. The stain on the one hand accounts for a certain agency of the subject to prefigure its own image, and on the other hand illustrates the body's dependency on its designated representational field. Silverman stresses the stain's importance in helping us understand how the body can corporeally assimilate the image and thus how flesh can be transformed into representation.

The subject's approximation of, or its failure to approximate, its surroundings leads to the Lacanian concept of mimicry, which in my analysis of Mapplethorpe becomes especially pertinent: here we encounter the notion of the image as a thrown-off skin. This idea, Silverman says, "connotes an *excretion* of the image, a refusal to 'wear' the 'photograph' through which one has been ratified as subject. This image of bodily dismemberment is evocative of the ways in which Frantz Fanon speaks about his rejection of the screen of 'blackness'" (ibid: 202, my emphasis). In connection with Mapplethorpe's photographs and Ivo's dance performance, the metaphor becomes relevant due to its function as a protective shield or a tool for seduction, which acts as an intermediary between the subject and the world of spectators. I want to imagine Mapplethorpe's images as just such a thrown-off skin, which allows his subjects to position themselves at some distance from their representations. Similarly, when Ivo stages his blackness with such insistence that one is fearful of being accused of focusing exclusively on Ivo's racial features, his skin is effectively thrown off through the image he presents of himself. Ivo dresses himself in white clothes and thus presents his skin as a guise, which he dons at will. The skin's blackness becomes the image that is presented. The skin and Ivo's body lie beneath the layer of representation and act from behind the invisible screen, somewhere beyond the photographic image. In a sense, Ivo refuses to wear Mapplethorpe's photograph – he excretes it.

Silverman's term *excretion* seems similar to Phelan's representational excess. Both connote forms of representational surplus. For Silverman, excretion is something to be discarded, to be thrown in the face of stereotyping reality. For Phelan, excess is invisible: something that representation conveys but we fail to see. This invisible substance makes possible resistant readings of the visual world, a process that Phelan ascribes to Mapplethorpe's self-portraits. She observes:

The image of the self, Mapplethorpe suggests, can only be glimpsed in its disappearance. To greet it, one risks blindness, vanishing. ... The image captured by the camera is an image, which is performed in order to define the central absence of the self-image. (40)

The absence of the self-image is here the excess of what representation conveys, and, in Phelan's analysis, a necessary self-criticism by Mapplethorpe as photographer. In my view, however, there is a discrepancy between the disappearance and the absence of self-image. The former is constituted by an initial presence of the imaged subject and its subsequent move toward invisibility; this is where Phelan positions her notion of excess. The latter is characterized by a fundamental nonappearance or nonexistence within the image, from which a hitherto neglected self can possibly emerge. This latter option is the assumption behind Silverman's argument about the pose.

In her detailed discussion of Cindy Sherman's *Untitled Film Stills* (1977-80), Silverman gives an account of how the pose is employed in Sherman's photography to convey the abyss between the self and an idealized image. Sherman's images suggest the "good-enough" photograph, in which the ideal woman, housewife, tragic heroine, or nature girl, is only partially approximated. Similar to the stain, the pose is worn or assumed by the body, and constitutes the body's "image-ability." If one poses for a photograph, one freezes, as if to imitate the image one is about to become. Or, as Barthes writes in *Camera Lucida* (1982): "I constitute myself in the process of 'posing', I instantaneously make another body for myself, I transform myself in advance into an image. ... I feel that the Photograph creates my body or mortifies it ..." (10-11).

Sherman excessively stages both the creation and the mortification of the body through the photograph within the photograph. She transposes the pose into the image, making the act of posing part of the composition, and so achieves a doubling of the look that is directed at the represented women. The look consequently resides within, as well as outside of, the image. This doubling of the look results in a seeing of oneself being seen. The viewer of the photograph also sees the depicted subject's exposure to the camera (gaze) and is implicated in the spectacle of the world. In that way, we are thus reminded of the alterity of the gaze, which, contrary to the look, issues from all sides and constitutes or shatters the looking subject through the click of an imaginary camera. In this sense, Sherman's photographic looks expose their viewer to an awareness of the gaze, which, in Silverman's view, marks and possibly opposes a subject's position within the field of vision, and which, in Lacanian theory, dissolves or blurs the contours of this subject's position. Lacan writes: "[If] I am anything in the picture, it is always in the form of [the stain]." (1978: 97)

In engaging with Sherman's *Untitled Film Stills* and what she calls their ability to produce a *Nachträglichkeit* (deferred action), Silverman optimistically maintains "the possibility of productive vision – of an eye capable of seeing something other than what is given to be seen, and over which the self does not hold absolute sway" (1996: 227). In my analysis of Mapplethorpe's *Self-Portrait* and Ivo's dance performance I hope to reveal a similarly productive vision, albeit one that leans more toward how Lacan theorizes the effect of the gaze. Silverman suggests that the camera/gaze photographically frames us within representation. Conversely, when photographed we feel "subjectively constituted, as if the resulting photograph could somehow determine 'who' we are" (ibid: 135). Although Lacan also uses the camera as a signifier for the gaze and posits its constitutive function for subjectivity, he also insists that the gaze takes on an object-like quality and that, always already residing in the image, it looks back at the viewer. The gaze thus involves the viewer in the image. And by creating a blind spot where the spectator's look looks back at her, it disrupts the subject's fixed viewing position. If we can say that the gaze for Lacan resides in the object, we might, adding to Silverman's productive looking, ascribe a transformational power to particular images. I believe, however, that this power can come into play only under the condition in which the gaze of the other is made visible (present) in and through the image.

Here, the argument ties in with Silverman's analysis of Sherman's art, as well as with my reading of Mapplethorpe. Both artists show something within their images that makes their beholder become aware of her unstable subject-position when confronted with a particular vision. Sherman's overemphasized pose in the images makes the viewer of her photographs rethink her own posing and accommodation of stereotypical images without ever really approximating them. Mapplethorpe's blurred look in the self-portrait indicates the viewer's own indistinct or indeed obscured viewing position. In both cases, time is visibly frozen in the image and reminds the viewer of the absence of motion and flexibility in representation. At the same time, the beholder might feel an urge to break the fixed position of the image, which she might do simply by looking or walking away from it. The spell of the pose is broken for the moment, but will return at the next click. Mapplethorpe's and Sherman's images hold onto and embrace a vision that is absent from non-pictorial consciousness. And they do what Silverman ascribes to the look's potentially transformative powers: they "confer the active gift of love upon bodies which have long been accustomed to neglect and disdain" (ibid: 227). Through the photographs they explore the tension between the pictorial body and the lived body – a tension that, I claim, is decisive for how we see particularly neglected bodies in and through a picture. In the next section I will consider this tension and its possible effect on viewing Mapplethorpe's black male model Ken Moody in a portrait from 1985.

THE UNCONSCIOUSLY VISIBLE

Mapplethorpe's portrait (Fig. 8) shows a side view of Ken Moody's upper body and head. Moody's head is turned toward the viewer, so that he looks out of the picture at her. The work looks like a black-and-white image with a black background, which seems to invade the scarce light that shines on the model's face and bare skin. Moody is enveloped in black, and his dark skin turns a cold, bluish white in contrast to the surroundings. At the right side of the image shines a thin, sharp-edged, and pointed golden leaf. The only truly colored element in the image, the "leaf" has an ephemeral, immaterial quality. It may be a part of a plant, it could also be a streak of light, or an illuminated crack in the solid black wall of the image's background, or an optical illusion, something that seems to move, imbued with magic. The colored crack of light in the background might also have resulted from the opening of a black curtain. This interpretation would suggest a stage-like setting and posit a strong link to movement and, in the context of my discussion here, to Ivo's dance.

Fig. 8: Ken Moody

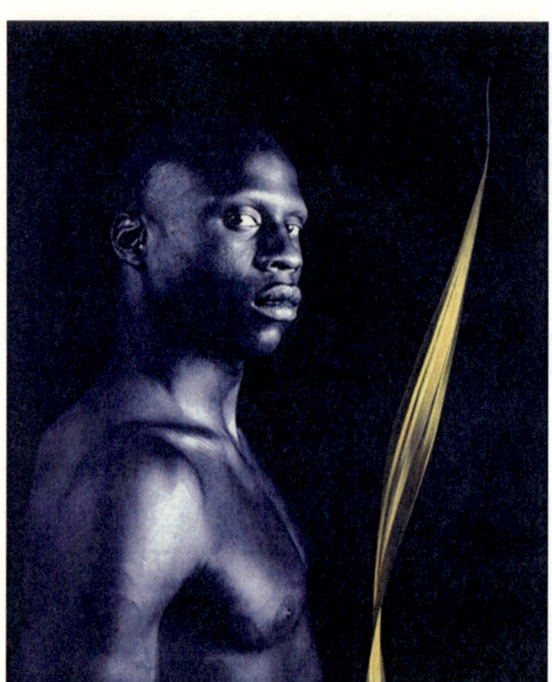

Source: Robert Mapplethorpe (1985), © Robert Mapplethorpe Foundation

Moody's hairless body, his well-defined muscles, large eyes, and sensual
lips make him one of Mapplethorpe's typical black males, which have been
discussed by art critics, political spokespersons, and cultural theorists with
reference to racial issues. [10] The racial and aesthetic dimension of
Mapplethorpe's imagery, it has been argued, reduce black male bodies to
abstract visual things, silence them as subjects, and put them in the service
of the artist's sexual fantasies. Carl Van Vechten, who like Mapplethorpe

---

10 Cultural critic Kobena Mercer has written two essays on his ambivalent
relationship to Mapplethorpe's photographs of black men, of which the later
text (1991) revises the critique put forth in the earlier article (1986), written
with filmmaker Isaac Julien. See Mercer and Julien 1986: 57-61, and Mercer
1991: 184-97.

was white and gay and was similarly fascinated by the black male body, has also been accused of foregrounding "the body of the other – as object of ridicule or admiration, as object of domination or commodification" (Jordan and Weedon, cited in Smalls 2006: 122). Kobena Mercer initially objected to Mapplethorpe's art for fetishizing the black male body in 1986 but later revised his views:

[what] is represented in the pictorial space of Mapplethorpe's photographs is a "look," or a certain "way of looking," in which the pictures reveal more about the absent and invisible white male subject who is the agent of representation than they do about the black men whose beautiful bodies we see depicted. (1991: 186)

Mercer's reassessment of Mapplethorpe's art engages with the images themselves, rather than focusing on the mere fact that a white artist has photographed nude, exposed, and sexualized black men. Also, Mercer acknowledges his own implication in the images as a (black) gay man, someone who, like a white spectator, is invested in desiring the object and who inhabits the same position of visual mastery he attributes to the hegemonic white male subject.

In the popular and politicized discourse about Mapplethorpe's art, the controversy concentrated on what, to an aesthetically trained Western eye, was the disruptive – because expressively beautiful – photographic presence of black bodies in artistic imagery. The discussion did not take into account the ambivalent power of the images and their cultural embeddedness in a specific logic of the gaze, a gaze through which the viewer as well as the photographed subject is either socially constituted or negated as spectacle. Although I believe that such political debate is necessary, I contend that the problem lies beyond the disparity between black and white skin color. What matters is how Mapplethorpe, in Mercer's words, "reveals what is 'unconscious' in the cultural construction of whiteness as a 'racial' identity" (ibid: 195). The portrait of Moody brings to the fore the construction of blackness.

Moody's skin in the photograph is not, strictly speaking, black. Reflecting the pale light, the skin acquires a lucid gleam. The golden-brown leaf, the only colored element, adds to the effect of uncertainty about the model's skin color. Offering the viewer only a splash of real color, it indicates the absence of Moody's skin color. The only actual sign of dark skin is its contrast to the whites of Moody's eyes. Hence, in this portrait, the black body that is supposed to be there cannot really be seen. Moreover, the leaf makes the viewer aware of the real body's absence from the photograph. The body that is visible is the mere abstraction of memorized and culturally reinforced images of a black body.

In his essay "A Small History of Photography" (1931), Walter Benjamin observes "how much easier it is to get hold of a picture, more particularly of a piece of sculpture, not to mention architecture, in a photograph than in reality" (1979: 253).[11] Remarkably, Benjamin does not mention the human body in his text, an omission all the more conspicuous because he may have been aware of the paradoxical relationship of photography to live bodies. Belting explains Benjamin's statement as follows: "Da Bilder traditionell das Abwesende sichtbar machen, kompensiert man die Unsicherheit über den Körper mit seiner Präsenz im Bilde, womit sich der übliche Sinn einer Abbildung umkehrt" (2000: 178). Images make visible what is absent, and to compensate for the body's representational uncertainty, image-makers stress its presence in the image more forcefully. This process consequently inverts the meaning of *Abbild*, which literally means the depiction *of* something; but here the body is made into an image. This inversion of referentiality is reminiscent of my discussion of the body's absence in the image above. One might come to the conclusion that there exists a fundamental incongruity between image and body.

Yet, as has become pertinent with regard to Ivo's dance performance, the problem of the body's absence in the image lies not so much in a mutual inaptness between body and image as in the split between live bodies and the image-producing vision of the viewer. What Ivo's mirror scene exposes is the representational absence of a specific *kind* of body. Ivo's black body appears only through the insistent presentation of his dark skin and his nudity: his body is stripped of cultural artifact, fashion, fabric, and other markers of various representational economies. In this raw state, Ivo sees himself fragmented and split through the white mirror. When the dancer is slowly transformed into a whitened figure, his state of

---

11 "Jeder wird die Beobachtung haben machen können, wieviel leichter ein Bild, vor allem aber eine Plastik, und nun gar Architektur, im Photo sich erfassen lassen als in der Wirklichkeit" (Benjamin, 1991: 381-2).

disintegration (or disidentification?) subsides and he becomes less and less visible to his audience. I want to suggest that Ivo's dance shows us that every living body, and especially marked bodies, are absent from the images that are produced by what Belting calls ideologies or cultural fictions of the body. In this sense, images of the body are necessarily linked to a culturally constructed image-efficiency or image-ability. Ultimately, Belting suggests, there is little to gain from doubting the body's qualities (*Zweifel am Körper*), while one must certainly doubt the ability of images to represent the living body – indeed, the black, the female, the queer, and the disabled body (*Zweifel an der Bildfähigkeit*; ibid: 178).

What I conclude from these observations, partly against Benjamin's argument, is that the body is more difficult to grasp in a photograph, because it dies in the image. It disappears from view, and only under rare conditions does it leave a vague trace on exposed film, as with Mapplethorpe's smear. But in what way is Mapplethorpe's shadow comparable to Ivo's tracing of images of black bodies?

When Benjamin refers to Karl Blossfeldt's plant photographs, he insists that photographs, in contrast to paintings, produce a magical value that urges the viewer to search for a hitherto undiscovered existence (1979). The pictures depict plants in such detail that they suggest human-made forms like ancient columns, women's dresses and brochures, slightly askew minarets, or industrial iron springs. Benjamin ascribes to these photographs the capacity to make unknown or invisible existences meaningful. Similarly, Mapplethorpe's ephemeral leaf-like object points to a new meaning for human skin color: the leaf attracts and drains all the brown and ocher particles from the image, leaving most of the image in darkness, and tinting Moody's skin a colorless grey.

What we can or cannot commonly perceive is defined by what is not representable, what does not figure as a culturally readable visual sign. To explain the after-image as an absent, unrepresentable, yet visible phenomenon, Phelan draws on Benjamin's notion of the optical unconscious:[12]

---

12 Benjamin describes the veiled aspect of consciousness – which is, importantly, not a psychological but a perceptual consciousness – through reference to the process of walking. Walking reveals something about our bodily consciousness without revealing anything about the body. Benjamin writes: "Whereas it is a

[The] after-image participates in a kind of "optical unconscious" (the phrase is Walter Benjamin's) – a realm in which what is not visibly available to the eye constitutes and defines what is – in the same way as the unconscious frames ongoing conscious events. Just as we understand that things in the past determine how we experience the present, so too can it be said that the visible is defined by the invisible. (1992: 14)

Benjamin acknowledges the existence of a visual space informed by the unconscious, a hidden part of reality that photography reveals through its devices of slow motion, enlargement, or extended exposure. Below I will refer to Eadweard Muybridge's "instantaneous photographs": photographic studies in which the photographer tried to depict moving bodies through a series of still images.

Benjamin ascribes to a number of early-twentieth-century photographs the capacity to produce a vivid and lasting impression on the viewer because of the long period of exposure that used to be necessary to develop an identifiable portrait. Due to the time lapse involved in production, the process also resulted in an absence of contact between image-making and actuality. The process allowed the sitter to grow into the picture and give it an air of permanence, so that later the viewer is urged to bridge the photographed (absent) past and the chemically (artificially) developed present in the beheld image. Benjamin's account of the subsequent development of commercial portrait photography, however, registers a sense that the magic of earlier photographs has disappeared. He cites Bertolt Brecht's observation that "less than ever does the mere reflection of reality reveal anything about reality" (Benjamin 1979: 255).

How does Benjamin's concept of the optical unconscious and its miraculous effect on the viewer bear on Mapplethorpe's photography? Michael Taussig's interpretation, mainly concerned with the physiognomic aspects of the visual world, stresses Benjamin's confounding of subject and object. He explains:

commonplace that ... we have some idea what is involved in the act of walking ... we have no idea at all what happens during the fraction of a second when a person steps out" (Benjamin 1979: 243).

For what came to constitute perception with the invention of the 19th-century technology of optical reproduction of reality was not what the unaided eye took for the real. No. What was revealed was the optical unconscious – a term that Benjamin willingly allied with the psychoanalytic unconscious but which, in his rather unsettling way, so effortlessly confounded subject with object such that the unconscious at stake here would seem to reside more in the object than in the perceiver. He had in mind both camera still shots and the movies, and it was the ability to enlarge, to frame, to pick out detail and form unknown to the naked eye, as much as the capacity for montage and shocklike abutment of dissimilars, that constituted this optical unconscious which, thanks to the camera, was brought to light for the first time in history. (1991: 149)

Taussig's reading interprets the optical unconscious as a tactile quality of seeing, through which habitual knowledge is brought to bear on the visible world. Taussig locates habitual ways of knowing in the everyday experience of touch: "The tasks facing the perceptual apparatus at turning points in history, cannot ... be solved by optical, contemplative, means, but only gradually, by habit, under the guidance of tactile appropriation" (ibid: 149).

If looking is informed by other senses, and if these senses are influenced by technology, photography not only brought into view what had hitherto been unconscious, but it also changed the relationship between the seer and the seen. The seer as photographer became invisible behind the camera; the seen as sitter was thus perceived through a material object rather than a human eye. Yet, at the same time, the model had the (restricted) freedom to pose for an objective eye or for herself. The camera's object, which in portrait photographs is represented by a person or a living body, consequently seems to embody and radiate a particular, yet unconscious, knowledge about the vision of which she is part. With Mapplethorpe's self-portrait, it seems that the image itself, and not Benjamin's view of it, confounds the notions of subject and object: it exposes Mapplethorpe to the camera's eye as an object of his own technological, white male (sexualizing) gaze.

In his work on the mirror stage, Lacan identifies a fundamental moment, at which the infant sees herself as both the subject before the mirror (recognition) and the object reflected in the mirror (misrecognition). This double seeing of the self is reminiscent of Benjamin's confounding of the photograph's subject and object. If we take the subject-object concurrence as something that bears on Ken Moody's portrait, this may stir up a critical relationship between the objectified black model and the white man's vision.[13] Can Moody overturn the borders between subjecthood and objecthood, as Mapplethorpe does in his self-portrait? Ivo's mirror scene shows that, before it can challenge the mode of production in which bodies are seen, Moody's body will always be an image of a black man and, receding into darkness, it is becoming invisible. This disappearing is, as Belting observed, ultimately caused by the absence of subjectivity in the image. The photograph might, under certain conditions, have the capacity to transform the precarious relation between body, subjectivity, and image. To understand what these conditions might be, I will thematize the process of a subject's becoming an image.

MODES OF BECOMING IMAGE

In his essay "Wild Laughter in the Throat of Death" (1987), Jean-Luc Nancy writes about a Charles Baudelaire poem about the desire to paint the image of a woman. Nancy describes this desire as the desire to paint the endless process of forming an image, of imagining. The desire of the poet/artist is not

[to] have or produce an image, but to be the image [himself], or ... the imagining process, the process of becoming-an-image. It is the desire to come – as an image, to be the coming (to appearance) of an image. This does not mean representing oneself ... Instead, it means becoming the specific movement of the image becoming image, the becoming visible of the visible, the coming (to appearance) of visibility ... The desire to paint [is] to be presenting everything not as a copy or portrait, but as the disappearance of everything in its own presence. (Nancy 1987: 727-28)

In portraiture, the subject of the painting eludes imitation. As Nancy observes, the painted woman becomes the "painting of a woman." In other

---

13 Winnubst (2004) criticizes Lacan's conception of the mirror stage for disregarding racialized bodies; she considers it important to ask if the "mirror is racist."

words, the painted subject grows into the image and presents itself from within itself, from behind itself. This conception suggests a critique of the subject-object relation between painter and sitter, and indicates a new form of imaging/imagining. The painted woman turns into a presence of her own making. She becomes a subject with a voice that asks to be painted. At the same time, because she represents the *becoming* of the image instead of a woman's image, her image as *Abbild*, the copy of her real body, disappears.

In portrait painting, as characterized by Nancy, the painted model disappears from the image: her face disappears into the material of the paint, into the colors; and, in Nancy's example, into the woman's "laughter," which Baudelaire describes as her "wide mouth, red and white and alluring, that makes one dream of the miracle of a superb flower blooming on a volcanic soil" (cited in Nancy 1987: 720). Nancy reads or perceives the painted mouth as laughter, as an expression that cannot be "seen," but that is the only part of the painted woman that does not disappear from the image, because it is not subjected to the laws of representation. The model's laughter becomes the only positive presence in the image. It survives representation because it indicates something beyond the visual: it is not dependent on color, light, or shade, or on the substance of the painting. The woman's laughter is present in the image, yet transcends the material conditions of it. Nancy calls this the "wild laughter in the throat of death." Metaphorically, the laughter is born from the vanishing life of the model in representation.[14]

If Nancy's theory can be transferred to Mapplethorpe's portrait of Ken Moody, the abstracted laughter might in this case reside in the look. Unlike the woman's laughter in Nancy's example, a representation of her unheard voice, Moody's look represents the model's ethereal, invisible, or unseen view. The large eyes framed by black shadows represent the loss of his body to the looks of the outside world. The black man's body, lost in representation, confronts the spectator with a model of Moody's absent real body. His individual body disappears from the image, and what takes its place is the force, the sensation of his look. The look survives

---

14 Nancy calls painting a "metaphor for all the arts to the extent that they are supposed to represent." He then goes further: "'Painting' represents representation in general" (Nancy 1987: 731).

representation, leaves the picture, and becomes alive in the viewer's perception.

The perceptual transfer from the model's look in the image to the viewer's perception beyond the image reflects Nancy's formulation of the painting that comes into appearance only through the movement of the image becoming image. Moody's transgressive look not only accomplishes this movement, it also doubles the photographed look, which comes to reside in and outside of the picture.

The movement of the image becoming image entails a doubling of the image, but not, as in Eadweard Muybridge's stop-motion photographs, in the form of a repetition or an almost identical multiplication. Muybridge became known in the late nineteenth century for his attempts to capture realistic motion on photographic film. His pictures typically show a line-up of stills made of subjects in motion, such as a woman walking down the stairs. Yet the images do not convey movement unless they are animated in a sequence. Without being able to see or feel the time-gap in between the making of each of the images, the viewer does not see moving bodies but only an abstraction of movement.

A contemporary attempt to capture the movement of bodies in a different way was made by the artist David Michalek in his piece *Slow Dancing* (2007). The series of 43 larger-than-life, hyper-slow-motion video portraits of dancers and choreographers was projected on the façade of the Lincoln Center in New York City in July 2007. Muybridge used only a few photographic images to show motion; Michalek records thousands of sequential video images to indicate the idea of stillness. The moving image here is slowed down to such a degree that one can barely perceive the bodies' gestures. In both works movement is reconsidered: it becomes dependent on the viewer's perception and is not seen as an inherent characteristic of an animate object or organism.

Both photographs discussed in this chapter make the movement of an image-becoming-image visible through, precisely, the display of time's absence. The absence of time in Mapplethorpe's art could be one of the problematic elements in his display of black bodies, since it also entails a certain negation or loss of historical perspective in his vision of racially othered bodies, which, perhaps unintentionally but also unreflectively reproduces historically problematic views.

Mapplethorpe's ghostly smear of light, which becomes a blurred, Francis Bacon–like smirk, reveals the lengthened exposure of photographic film needed to produce such an image. And Moody's upper body, sculpted like a statue carved in stone, forever still, is set in one frame with the volatile, elusive shape of obscure – and possibly inhuman – nature. Time cannot be experienced here as a positive presence. It brings the images to life no more than Muybridge's "still lifes" do. But, as Bayard aimed to effect with his portrait of himself as deceased, the images of Mapplethorpe bring into perspective the consequences and the restraints of passing and past time. When the movement of time is missing from an image, when time is captured in a still image, it shows the mortifying effect of the pose (Barthes 1982) in any form of representation.

In bringing time in photography into view, Mapplethorpe not only contorts the image of himself as a representative of the white gaze – a gaze now mirroring itself while caught in misty prejudice – but he also indicates the un-realness of bodily representation. The fixed image of a black male body is unveiled as a visual construction, an imaginary version of the real black male body. Mapplethorpe depicts the danger of the repetition of imagery that neglects the body's predisposition for transformation and its potential for difference.

The subversion of the rigid representation of the othered black, female, disabled, or queer body requires a splitting of the existing image into two or more image-like visions that, on the one hand, inescapably represent the gaze of Western hegemonic ideology, and, on the other, crucially, the self-seeing view of the othered subject. The split image in Mapplethorpe's photographs, as well as the fragmented image in Ivo's performance, resides within, not outside of, the original representation. They materialize as a distorted, partial, or, as in Moody's portrait, non-human overlay.

This idea of the overlay can be understood within Phelan's theory of absence as an excess of representation. But, contrary to Phelan's contention that excess lies outside of the image, here it appears to be a feature of the image itself – a usually absent feature that, under certain conditions, becomes visible. Again, we are reminded of Bayard's photographic technique of extended exposure, which created a vision of him that otherwise would not have been possible. With the help of the aging process of the film, Bayard facilitated an invisible or fictitious presence to grow into the image. The absence of some bodies in representation can thus possibly be compensated by a different reading of visual content: a reading that considers the fact that in an image something might be present, yet invisible. The absence of certain forms of visibility is, as we have seen, not so much, or not only, a problem of image-making but of image-*reading*. Again, as I proposed in chapter two, some images remind us of our failed vision (partial blindness), and some make us consider the potentially positive effects of this failure by guiding us to see the absence of visual presence.

5 Mirroring Age

[The] body is understood as an image –
something that is a resemblance or
likeness, a mirroring.

MIKE FEATHERSTONEIST

[Il] faudrait savoir ce que serait le *moi*
dans un monde où personne se saurait rien
de la symétrie par rapport à un plan.

JACQUES LACAN

A look at British photographer Antony Crossfield's *Narcissus* (2008) reveals two heads, a twisted torso, and a number of naked arms and legs that form an indecisive mass of human flesh in the midst of a bare and shabby room (Fig. 9). The amassed body parts are dimly mirrored in a puddle of dark green liquid on the floor. Two faces as well as an altered intersection of those same bodies emerge from the patch of reflecting ooze. The floral tapestry of the walls is stained and scratched, the radiator behind the two figures rusted and seemingly broken. An old tape recorder on the right and two partly unwound tapes on the left side of the dirty tile floor give the impression of an abandoned documentation project. Memories of a concluded past, recorded on analogue media, seem to have been discarded, dispersed in a space of incipient corporeal development. The heap of flesh on the floor consists of two male bodies that seem to grow out of each other. They are intimately intertwined, touching as much of the other's surface and insides as they would if they were Siamese twins. Their heads are turned toward their reflections on the floor.

Fig. 9: Narcissus

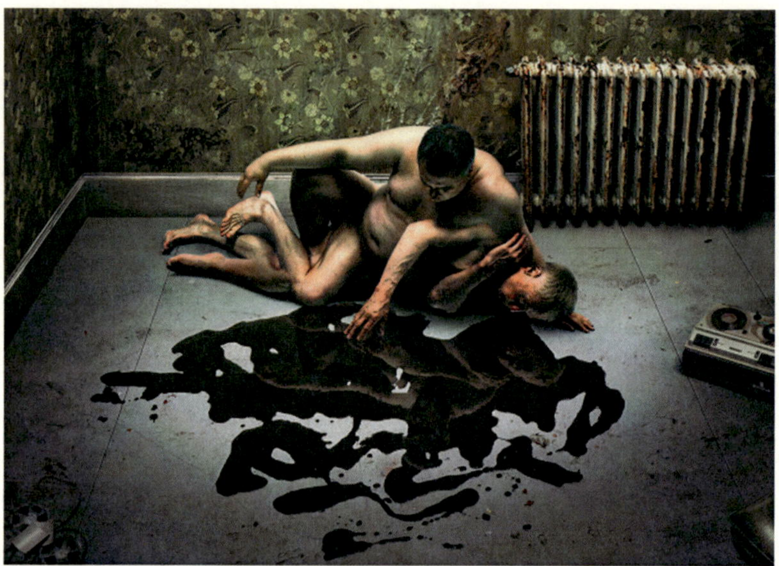

Source: Antony Crossfield (2008), Klompching Gallery & Mito Gallery

One man tenderly holds his fingertips just above his mirrored right hand and watches himself do it. His fingers do not disturb the smooth surface, while his protruding veins expose the effort of suspending his arm in midair. Comfortably resting one arm on his bent knee, the other man contemplates the reflected scene.

I introduce Crossfield's photograph at the beginning of this chapter so as to rethink and repicture both the figure of Narcissus and the mirror stage, suggesting a manner of self-relation that would offer an alternative to those powerful models. In contrast to my reflections on narcissism and the mirror stage in chapter three, where I proposed the potential productivity resulting from one's losing, instead of forming, one's self in the mirror, I will here focus on the idea that the assumed symmetry between the self and her acquired body-image in the mirror stage is precarious, yet also transformational. I here shift my attention to the potential failure of the mirror to form our aging selves, which, as I contend, are misled by the body-images we learned to form in infancy. Crossfield's image helps to problematize the function of the mirror stage and the conceptualization of the body-image by introducing new features into three aspects: age, intimacy, and horizontality. Crossfield's Narcissi are not young but old, they are not solitary but intimate, and they reflect themselves not vertically but horizontally.

Crossfield's photograph shows us age, intimacy, and horizontality in a way that helps me to reflect on identity after and beyond Lacan's mirrored subject (Lacan 2006: 75-81).[1] I want to try to analyze the possibility of forming positive versions of what the American age theorist Margaret Morganroth Gullette has called "aging identities" (124: 2004).[2] Because Crossfield's photographic account of the myth of Narcissus severs the necessary and seemingly unproblematic link between the incipient self and the mirror, I find the image useful for developing a theory of the aging body in productive terms, which would account for not only the development over time of the subject's inner self, but also the significance of the subject's changing body, which in time outgrows the once-defined mirrored body-image. Crossfield's work suggests an expansion of psychoanalytic conceptions of the subject's identity-formation through the solitary (or parentally and socially monitored) look into a vertical mirror. He adds a second body besides Narcissus's aged and naked visual presence in the picture, and moreover rotates the whole scene onto a horizontal plane, traditionally associated with the intimate sphere of two partners' lovemaking, or perhaps more negatively with the sickbed of the elderly, those individuals who are almost ageless, are in fact closer to infants than to adults, and have been expelled from the normative world of those of upright posture. The double Narcissus displayed here provokes a new look at the formation of aged selves with aged bodies. Crossfield narrates the event of self-recognition in the mirror in a new way, thus telling another mirror-story. In my eyes, the picture puts forward a fresh bodily narrative that is cognizant of age, and that, in its picturing of a poignant relationship between our bodies and our culturally mirrored body-images, may indeed concern all subjects – young and old, male and female, small and big. In this sense, the work challenges the discriminatory "age-gaze" (Gullette 2004: 161-62) of traditional theories of subject formation by showing the viewer an alternative, and possibly queer, version of the mirror stage.

---

1   See also my discussion of Lacan's theory of the mirror stage in chapter 3.

2   Gullette notes that this term was already commonly used by gerontologists.

In this chapter, I aim to explore body-images from the perspective of later life. Starting with the earliest conscious encounter of our self-seeing as an infant during the mirror stage, yet now exploring it from an aged point of view, I want to counter what we can call the decline-value of psychoanalytic and Western cultural body narratives. The visual separation of the child from the mother in the mirror phase not only leads to subject formation, but also contains the potential danger of conflating one's sense of self largely or merely with one's mirror image. By tracing the concepts of the *specular body*, the *speculative body*, and the *performative body* in relation to Crossfield's photograph, joined below by a sculpture by Robert Gober (*Untitled*, 1990), I attempt to examine the mirror's incapacity to reflect aged body-images positively. I consider the idea of a reversed mirror-phase, which may broaden Lacan's conception of and our perspective on the body's vital influence on the development of the self after infancy and youth.

Crossfield's photograph presents the viewer with a twisted version of a *specular body*. The specular (reflected) body is the physical self that others see and, in relation to the processes of aging, it is the body that is responsible for the narrative of decline, decrepitude, illness, weakness, and passivity. Crossfield, however, gives his specular bodies new visual agency by using *speculative photography* in Anca Cristofovici's sense, showing them as part of a speculative project (2009: 10). In *Touching Surfaces: Photographic Aesthetics, Temporality, Aging* (2009), Cristofovici defines speculative photography as an artistic practice that extends visibility and temporality through a variety of unconventional photographic techniques, such as digital editing or collage. She ascribes to this form of photography the ability to represent paradoxical perceptions of time and identity and to reshape our understanding of corporeal and mental realities (ibid: 63).

Through artistic means, the artist mediates (speculates on) the becoming self and presents the viewer with an internal mirror (speculum). Her work creates the idea of a *speculative body*, a body that cannot be represented in linear time or in accordance with binaries such as past and present or young and old. My conception of the speculative body is a body that incorporates paradoxical, uncertain, and provisional features; a body that is a collage of several bodies, objects, spaces, and gaps; a body that motivates a viewer to speculate about its properties and material substance.

Finally, in Crossfield's as well as Gober's artworks, the *performative body* emerges from the material of the artworks. Photography, as well as the wax Gober uses for his sculpture, are inevitably associated with dimensions of time, much like aging. The passing of time and constant change are conditions for the aliveness of art and human existence. Yet, photographs as well as aging materials and bodies are defined by the recording of, or a reference to, an earlier moment in time. Crossfield and Gober consequently present bodies to the viewer that will eventually "outlive" or leave their medium, since the material through which they are represented will not survive the firm grip the bodies are supposed to have on their ideal appearance in an unreachable past. In that way, the artworks touch the spectator's sense of corporeality by offering the conception of a deteriorating mirror instead of a decaying body. They might thus slightly modify the viewer's self-relation and body-image.

Crossfield's *Narcissus* displays obvious visual similarities to Caravaggio's *Narcissus*, such as the dark oily puddle on the floor, which, unlike an actual mirror, reflects the body/bodies in the form that suggests a relief or sculpture. The black paint in Caravaggio's work produces a thickness and depth that dissolves the hard flat surface of the mirror.[3] Crossfield's puddle looks as if it were perforating the floor, creating a deep hole, or we might say it resembles a sculptural fragment in high relief that pushes the mirrored figures out of the reflecting surface. The image of Narcissus thus gains liveliness and substantiality, doubling the "real" boy as sculpted human material. In Crossfield's photograph, the duplication becomes a quadruplication, producing a comparable effect. The manufactured carnality, or fleshiness, results in what Mieke Bal describes as the dissolution of the mirror's boundary in Narcissus's self-formation:

As Narcissus' body gets to know itself, it loses its boundary. Something along the way of this boy's mirror stage went wrong. At the four corners of the austere, self-enclosing rectangle, the sleeves, especially in their reflected form, seem icons of the water the disturbance of which will make Narcissus' image disappear. As Caravaggio represented him, Narcissus is suspended between the solidity that imprisons and the fluidity that dissolves; he is framed by his own body. (1999a: 242)

---

3   See Bal's analysis of Caravaggio's *Narcissus* in Bal 1999a: 231-61.

Crossfield's Narcissi are likewise close to transgressing the limits of their selves and crossing into the space beyond their reflections as one man's hand hovers close to the still surface, putting both men's self(-image) at risk by "muddying the water" (ibid: 242).

Crossfield's intertwined bodies also frame their self-image, yet do so in not as all-embracing fashion as does Caravaggio's Narcissus. The splattered puddle gives form to their image by imitating the bodies' entanglement. The scraggly confusion of extremities is replicated by the haphazardly spread liquid on the floor. Form is constructed here through chaos, as unity is through multiplication, living flesh through dead matter, the self through the other. This, I argue, amounts to a reverse process of Narcissus's ego formation. The matured "boys" do not experience the jubilation of the purported wholeness assumed by the infant. But they nonetheless engage in an intimate albeit different sort of communication with the mirror, robbing it of its powers. In place of the reflected mirror image, the "real" bodies take over the function of signification. Does Crossfield, like Caravaggio, show us and contaminate us with a collapse of narcissism (ibid: 246)? Did something go wrong in their mirror stage, too?

Bal suggests that Caravaggio confronts us with a reversed mirror stage (ibid: 245). I would like to argue that what went wrong in the mirror stage of Caravaggio's Narcissus is not the essential and productive "miscog nition" (*méconnaissance*) proposed by Lacan, but rather Narcissus's recognition that the mirror, any mirror, always already contains an image of himself and his body, even before he lays his eyes on it. This interpretation suggests that self-recognition and ego formation are threatened at a later life stage, not so much by the potential loss of one's body-image, but rather by the realization that whoever I am, I am (only) in view, or in the look, of the mirror; in other words, what I am is what I become when I meet my own reflection in a mirror that contains more than my inner sense of self. What I, as a matured person with an aged body, see in the mirror is the mirror's narrative, its cultural construction as constituent frame of my self. Turning my back toward the mirror becomes potentially dangerous because, by identifying the mirror's powers, I lose my imagined control over my body-image. Ovid's Narcissus thus sacrificed his life not necessarily for his self-love, but for fear of losing control over his sense of wholeness and unity.[4]

In contrast, Crossfield's Narcissi do not seem desperate or in pain to look at their mirror image. Instead of languishing in their reflection, they seem to engage lazily in a pleasurable visual conversation with their reflected counterparts, a process that has no temporal or spatial limitations. The dialogue displayed in this image is a constructive revocation of the infant's alleged mirror stage. Hence, Crossfield challenges Lacan's notion of self-formation. If, in Lacan's conception, the body-image as unity emerges from the body in bits and pieces, Crossfield's *Narcissus* suggests a different sort of emergence: of intimate and foreign (other) bodies as inherent parts of the self.

THE FOREIGN BODY

Crossfield's "Foreign Body" comprises a collection of images, in which two aged male bodies intersect in ways that make it unclear where one ends and the other begins. The borders of the figures dissolve. The composition of several digital images, taken of the same subjects at different times and from different angles, shows the body to be contingent on its surrounding space and its experience of lived time. The montage of the photographs suggests that several pictures were taken at different times in different settings and then merged. One picture adds to the next not only a new layer of visual content, but also an additional layer of time and space. The chronology governing these singular pictures is obscured, and the interior design of the photographic stage may well have been tampered with. The end result thus represents a real situation, with real bodies and real props, while also highlighting the uncertainty of their authenticity. The depicted bodies cannot be separated from the transformation of the spatial and

---

4   Sylvia Plath's poem "Mirror" (1961) dramatizes the power of the mirror over an aging woman by using the mirror as first-person narrator. The mirror's indisputable objectivity is cold and incapable of emotion. It swallows everything that it sees, and instead of reflecting back the woman's inner sense of self, it harshly focuses on her body's decay: "In me she has drowned a young girl, and in me an old woman / Rises toward her day after day, like a terrible fish" (Plath 2002: 173).

temporal frames of the digital project of the artist and are thus contingent upon their surroundings. Discussing these images on his website (www.antonycrossfield.com), Crossfield notes that they equate "the temporal and spatial indeterminacies of the bodies and selves they depict with the analogous fragmentation of photographic representation in a digital age where old certainties have been compromised."

The term "foreign body" is mainly used in physiology, where it designates an object that is external to an organic or mechanical organism and intrudes into the body in either inert or irritating ways. If in this context a foreign body commonly causes a disturbance in the system's functioning, in the context of Crossfield's art project it seems to play a different role, one that is beneficial or at least creative. Crossfield's reference to an ordinarily disturbing element suggests that the disturbance is dependent on whatever function is ascribed to the body, and that a "foreign body" might not only be destructive but also constructive for a human subject's self-image.

In creating a photographic print, analog photography uses a medium, photographic paper, that reacts to chemical processes so as to record visual information. The information conveyed by analog signals consists of a continuous response to changes in light and temperature, and is directly transposed to a physical medium. Digital photography records information discontinuously through image sensors that read the intensity of light. The captured data, converted in binary numeric form, are transferred onto a digital memory device and converted to digital images on a computer. Whereas in analog photography, the linear progress of time is essential to the capturing of information, in digital photography time's continuity can be ignored, through the recording of distinct, and possibly unrelated, moments. What is striking about Crossfield's images is that here analog and digital technologies seem to merge. The dilapidated and obviously aged settings of his photographs, as well as the wrinkles and sagging skins of his models, all work to convey a sense of the passing of time. Yet the digitally manipulated fusion of the bodies creates an impression of nonlinear reality. This suggests an ambiguous or anachronistic relation between the passing of time and the process of aging.

The Cartesian concept of a disembodied self is twisted here in several ways. Each subject finds itself in another subject's body, in a process that manifests and augments the self's physical dimensions, seeping into the space around the bodies, as in Narcissus's puddle. The rooms' décor and props display corporeal characteristics, exaggeratedly imitating the human body's inevitable tendency to decay and die. Rusted radiators suggest bared ribcages; cracks in the walls and flaking wallpaper bring to mind wrinkles and dried skin; old pipes and truncated cables look like protruding veins. The prominent presence of a typewriter, sewing machine, and tape recorder in some of the photographs seem to reference the body's dependency on mechanical technology as prosthesis, even in our digital age. A set of old photographic cameras superimposed in one image (*Foreign Body #5*) suggests how bodies see and are seen in a predesigned way (Fig. 10).

Fig. 10: Foreign Body #5

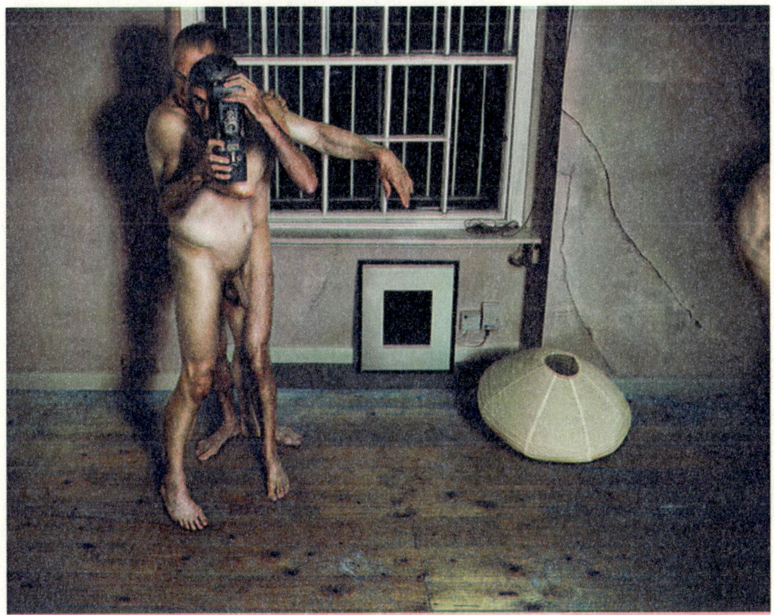

Source: Antony Crossfield (2006), Klompching Gallery & Mito Gallery

Frosted or blackened windows, large or small mirrors, and a half-transparent screen of cloth all suggest, as the artist describes it, "both a barrier and a display; a means of concealment and of revelation. [The screen] evokes the idea that the body is something that is projected upon, as much as something that hides what is within, and further suggests the breakdown of the distinctions between inside and outside" (Crossfield in Kouwenhoven 2010: 43). Crossfield's images challenge the existence of a border between mind and body, between self-image and mirror-image. The images projected onto the subjects' bodies pass through their skin and evolve in the subjects' self-perception, which is, partly, again propelled outwards. The body thus becomes a body with several layers, created in conjunction with other, foreign bodies.

Fig. 11: Screen (Foreign Body)

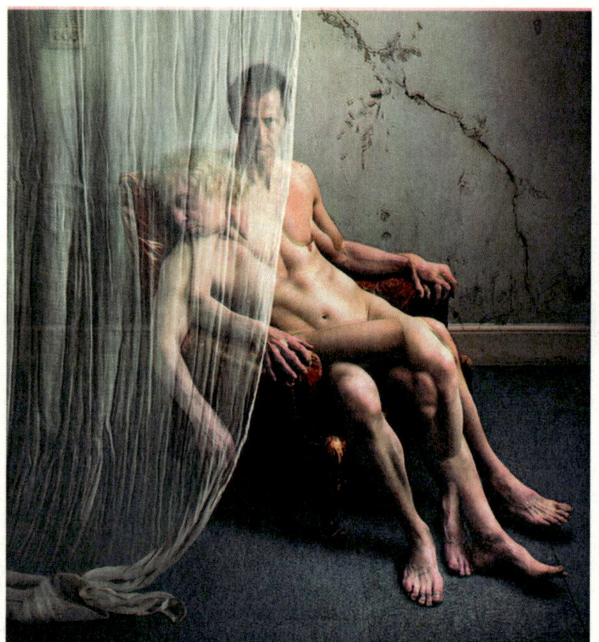

Source: Antony Crossfield (2009), Klompching Gallery & Mito Gallery

The conjoined body-mass in "Foreign Body" (Fig. 11) consists of more than one self. The four legs and arms, two heads and torsos accommodate a multiplicity of potential, shifting, and developing selves and sexes. Crossfield seems to aim at producing a fragmentary image that reads as a unitary photograph. He thus offers a visual metaphor for the illusion of wholeness that conceals a fundamentally fragmented self.

Fig. 12: Foreign Body #4

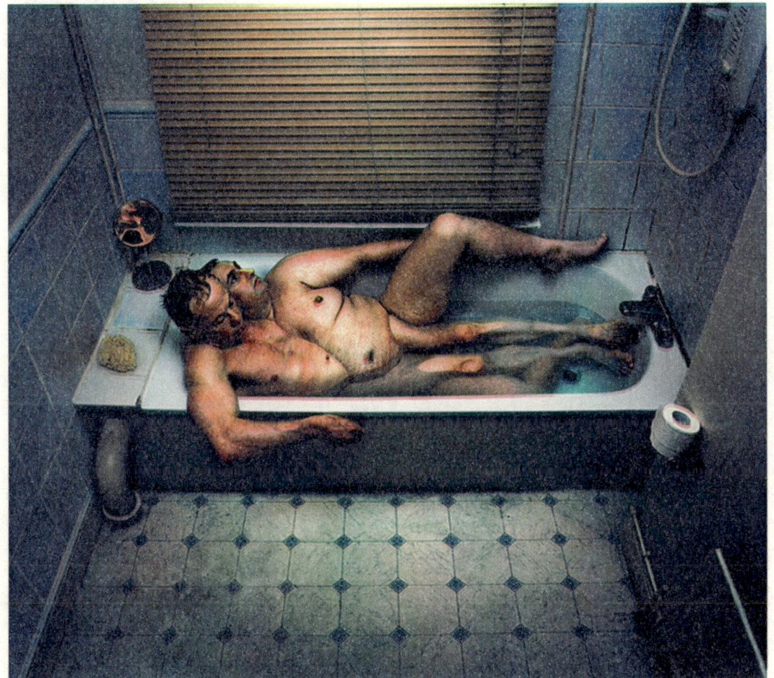

Source: Antony Crossfield (2005), Klompching Gallery & Mito Gallery

The merged figures seem to be masculine, but, in some of the images (see for example Figs. 12 and 13), their overlap conceals the obvious signs of biological maleness, the penis and the absence of breasts. What becomes visible instead alludes to the triangle of a woman's pubic hair, smooth female breasts, or the round and soft bottom of a younger woman. Sometimes, one man's leg stands in for the missing penis and creates an uncanny sight, shifting between there being a lack and a surplus of phallic anatomy. In contrast, the parts of the images not digitally altered reveal the sagging flesh, wrinkles, scars, skinny legs, large bellies, hairy soft male breasts, thinning scalps, and pimples of Crossfield's older male models. The two photographs that do show a penis give an unusually energetic impression. The two men are caught in different acts, recorded at different points of time, and the combination of their frozen movements exudes a vigor that seems greater than the singular acts of two individual actors. In other words, the models share one penis but possess the energy of two men. Each moves individually, one pulling away from or pushing toward the other, so that they seem to direct their combined body toward several aims within a single moment. This anatomical confusion exhibits human action and movement as not merely emerging from an individual body, but as being dependent on physical interactions, representing the simultaneous merging and clashing of different intentions and material conditions.

Fig. 13: Trap (Foreign Body)

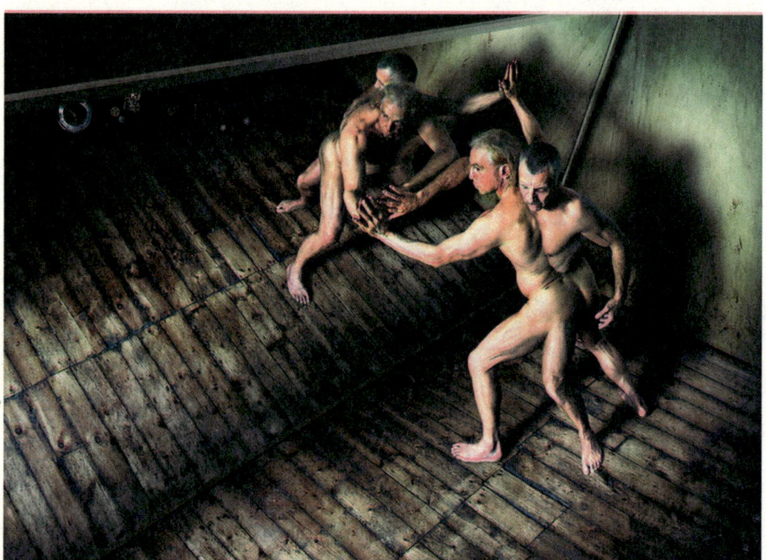

Source: Antony Crossfield (2009), Klompching Gallery & Mito Gallery

The sprawling torsos and limbs in Crossfield's *Narcissus* display a version of the myth of Narcissus that neither exhibits Narcissus's youthful beauty, nor performs his solitary self-reflection. Here, the mirror scene entails two aged male bodies, intricately interwoven and, through their reflection, in a constant visual dialogue with each other. Like the adolescent Narcissus, they seem to have become lost in their reflection; and like their younger counterpart, they might be in danger of drowning, of losing themselves, in the dark pool that gives the impression of a black hole in the floor.

In the mirror stage, the subject is simultaneously constituted by self-love and self-loss. The identification with the mirror image is an alienating process; yet it also forms the condition for relating to others. For Narcissus, in Ovid's myth, this process has not reached the productive and social stage. Young Narcissus remains stuck or lost in self-admiration; his (sexual) orientation toward others has yet to develop. Unlike their predecessor, however, the aged Narcissi's duplicity in Crossfield's photograph breaks the spell of perishing self-love. Through the presence of a second body, Narcissus' self-relating identity is disturbed. The mirror does not bestow on him his own image as exclusive love object, but directs his gaze to another person, a man, not quite like himself, but inseparably entangled with him. Self-love is still present, but only through another body's manifestation in the mirror.

REVERSE MIRROR STAGE

In an article on the literary imagination of old age, Kathleen Woodward postulates the "mirror phase of old age" (1983: 58). Woodward bases her idea on those of psychoanalyst Erik Erikson, who considers old age as distinct a phase in human life as infancy (1972), and on clinical psychological research, which suggests a critical relationship between elderly persons and their mirror images. The most extreme reaction to the mirror image is an aged person's radical rejection of her reflection. Sigmund Freud associates the perception of one's aged "double" with the uncanny: when one is surprisingly confronted with one's mirror image, one does not necessarily recognize it as one's reflection, yet it conveys something familiar that has been subdued.[5] Simone de Beauvoir connects the obsession with mirror images with aging, declaring that the knowledge of old age comes from the Other (within me) as well as from one's physical "decrepitude, ugliness and ill-health" (40). She writes:

---

5 In his essay on the uncanny, Freud tells a story about how, after having woken up with a start on a train trip and seeing his reflection in the window, he confused his mirrored double with an intruder into his compartment. He did not recognize himself and described this experience as uncanny (Freud 2003: 162, n III/1).

For the outsider it is a dialectic relationship between my being as he defines it objectively and the awareness of myself that I acquire by means of him. Within me it is the Other – that is to say the person who I am for the outsider – who is old: and that Other is myself. (284)

De Beauvoir describes the awareness of oneself as old through the look of someone else who regards one as old. Relating this idea to Woodward's theory, one can say that the self-recognition of an aged person takes place in the interaction between the mirror image (myself) and the gaze of the other (outsider).

De Beauvoir's argument suggests a resemblance between the mirror stage of infancy and what one could identify as the mirror stage of old age. The one can be seen as the inverse of the other. In both phases, the subject assumes an image by which it is transformed. The difference between the two stages lies in the type of transformation. While the infant experiences an incipient discrepancy between visual self-image and lived experience that leads to the anticipation of bodily wholeness, the aged person's interaction with the mirror image seems to move into the opposite direction, as Woodward proposes:

The harmonious whole resides within the subject, and the *imago* prefigures disintegration and "nursling dependence." If the infant holds his mirror image in an amorous gaze, the elderly person resists it. The narcissistic impulse remains – it imposes itself upon all our desires – but it is directed *against* the mirror image. (1983: 60)

The mirror stage of old age thus harbors a new form of narcissism, one that, by rejecting the subject's self-reflection, becomes a form of self-love that is beyond or even in opposition to visual pleasure. "Young" Narcissus desires his own vision; "old" Narcissus despises it. If we assume such an aged version of Narcissus to exist, what makes his narcissism blossom if not the visual pleasure gained from his own sight? Where, if not through vision, does he find love for himself?

For me, the figure of Narcissus in advanced age becomes a symbol for the general struggle with one's own body in relation to vision. The child's bliss in recognizing itself in the mirror reflects the satisfaction of anticipating its own body as whole, separate from the mother and the rest of the world. For the infant, body and self materialize and merge through visual recognition. For the aged subject, the gaze into the mirror separates the self from her body. As Woodward claims, "Old age is a state in which the body is in opposition to the self and we are alienated from our bodies" (1983: 55).

Crossfield's *Foreign Body* refers to alienation in age as well. But my understanding of Crossfield's images stands in contrast to Woodward's contention. Crossfield depicts alienation as a process that takes place between a subject's older and younger self and that productively allows for a form of intimacy between distinct (other, several) selves. The images postulate a new sense of self, less dependent on the image that was acquired time and again in the reenactment of the mirror stage, and more dependent on the interaction with other bodies.

That alienation is enforced through aging by the growing time-gap between the self's fantasized state *before* and the acquired ideal body-image *after* the mirror stage is stressed by Jane Gallop:

The jubilation, the enthusiasm [of the infant upon seeing itself in the mirror], is tied to the temporal dialectic by which she appears *already* to be what she will *only later become*. … The mirror stage itself is both an anticipation and a retroaction. (Gallop 1987: 78)

The mirror stage is a turning point from having a "body in bits and pieces" (Lacan 1953: 15) to acquiring a totalized image. Yet, as Gallop states, the mirror only retroactively brings forth the fantasy of a body in bits and pieces.[6] The violently shattered image is merely a projection or a reflection of the infant's becoming-self. There is nothing beyond the mirror. The mirror stage thus symbolizes a chronology of the developing self, which is fundamentally dependent on the fantasy of the "before." The achievement of, and the ensuing desire for, the self's "new" body-image is as much

---

6   "Laplanche and Pontalis thus seem to answer that the body in bits and pieces precedes the mirror stage. The mirror stage would seem to come after 'the body in bits and pieces' and to organize them into a unified image. But actually, that unorganized image only comes after the mirror stage so as to represent what came before. What appears to precede the mirror stage is simply a projection or a reflection. There is nothing on the other side of the mirror" (1987: 121).

based on the recognition of the infant in the mirror as on the idea of the self's emancipation from an earlier, shattered version of itself. Not only the self, but also "the body in bits and pieces" emanates from the mirror stage (Gallop 1987: 80). The temporality embedded in the mirror is perpetuated throughout a person's life. While the totalized image must continually be validated, the mirror trauma of the dismembered body accompanies every look into the mirror. Gallop emphasizes the importance of this temporal dialectic in its "violations of chronology," confirming the anachronistic nature of the body-image (1983: 121).[7]

To disrupt the idea of a natural formation of a subject's self, I want to add the concept of the "screen," which plays an important role in Lacan's theory of the gaze and which is interpreted by Kaja Silverman in her theory of vision. In *The Four Fundamental Concepts*, Lacan characterizes the screen as an imaginary mapping (1998: 107), which, as Silverman puts forward, is reminiscent of the infant's imaginary sense of mastery over its own body in the mirror stage (1992: 147). If the mirror is part of the imaginary order, the adult, on whom the child in fact depends on to be carried to the mirror, as Silverman stresses (ibid: 127), represents the symbolic order. The symbolic dimension of the mirror stage, which Lacan identifies as such only in his later work, corresponds to the gaze of the mother who watches the child seeing itself in the mirror. Silverman explains the child's self-recognition in the mirror by stressing the importance of the external gaze. She contends that the child's mirror experience is facilitated by, if not dependent on, the fact that the mother watches the child's self-seeing. The "seeing of oneself being seen" is a step toward the "seeing oneself seeing oneself" and constitutes the experience of the child's first sense of "self" (1992: 127).

The external gaze is thus a necessary component in the infant's identification and is later replaced by what Silverman calls the "dominant cultural screen" (ibid: 75): a repertoire of external images, which first comes in the form of the mirror reflection, subsequently via parental images, and later in the guise of a range of cultural representations. For Silverman, the exteriority of these images suggests that the subject

---

7   The loss of one's body-image occurs not only in aged subjects, but also in persons with eating disorders, physical disabilities, and transgender subjects. See Prosser in Stryker and Whittle: 94, 270).

becomes ever more dependent on the integration of what can be called "other" (1992: 56). The subject, Lacan writes, is not, however, "entirely caught up in this imaginary capture. He maps himself in it, [insofar] as he isolates the function of the screen and plays with it. ... The screen is here the locus of mediation" (1998: 107).

Complementing Lacan's concept of the subject's formation, Silverman insists upon

[the] social and historical [ideological] status of the screen by describing it as that culturally generated image or repertoire of images through which subjects are not only constituted, but differentiated in relation to class, race, sexuality, age, and nationality. (1992: 150)

This specification opens up the screen for political contestation, making agency visible in self-formation, along with the subject's capability of what Lacan calls "playing with the function of the screen" (1998: 107). At the same time, this function can serve as a defensive weapon or a shield. The screen thus intervenes within the subject's self-reflection. As helpful and necessary as this intervention might be for a developing child, it may be just as disruptive for an older person. In later life the screen might be the element that stands in the way of the subject's connection to her self-reflection and body-image.

I would like to suggest that the screen's grid, through which the subject is seen and sees itself, becomes denser and more opaque over a person's lifespan, hindering the aged person to recognize herself in the mirrored image on which identity is also conditioned. In Lacan's account, the screen is opaque by definition, necessarily so in order to see the pictures as we see them. As Lacan states, "if [the subject is] anything in the picture, it is always in the form of the screen" (1998: 97). However, Silverman stresses the screen's social and historical contingency to emphasize the subject's visual agency. If the subject is capable of playing with the function of the screen, she might be able to "exaggerate and/or denaturalize the image/screen; to use it for protective coloration; or to transform it into a weapon" (1992: 149). In addition to considering the screen as controlled protection, which even in Silverman's account is a rather bold and uncertain proposition, I want to suggest that the screen can be seen as becoming, with age, gradually *more* of (in Lacan's words) "a mask, a double, an envelope, a thrown-off skin, thrown-off in order to cover the frame of a shield" (1998: 107).

If the screen becomes denser with age, filling out and obscuring the mirror, the subject loses her body-image through the sheer overload of stereotypical, discriminatory, youth-glorifying, and gender-dividing images. It would be productive, therefore, to seek one's self-reflection outside or beyond the rectangular looking-glass. Here I see the constructive element in the idea of a reversed mirror stage in old age. When, according to such a concept, the subject starts disidentifying with her imaginary self in the mirror, the elderly person's look into the mirror becomes equivalent to the child's fantasy of a body in bits and pieces. As Crossfield's images show, this state of fragmentation is, however, not necessarily undesirable, since it potentially allows for a different and more intimate relationship with the other. The two bodies in Crossfield's *Narcissus* are intimately intertwined by way of yielding parts of their bodies to the respective parts of the other's body. Their fusion can take place only by means of an abandonment of a sense of wholeness.

Crossfield's image thus seems to suggest that the fragmented self can, at least in digital media or in visual fantasy, have a positive fragmented body-image. If, in Lacan's theory, the ideal ego formed in the mirror stage is a fiction (Lacan 2006: 94), and if there, as I propose, the specular (reflected) body becomes a speculative (multiple, uncertain) body, the formative process of becoming a subject is also a performative act of acquiring and admitting an image of oneself as partial, as linked to others, as aging. In this respect, subject formation can describe a continuous movement between seeing and identifying with one's specular body (acquired in the mirror stage of infancy, as seen by others) and accepting or even desiring the utopian nature of bodily wholeness (speculative body), which, as Crossfield shows, can playfully be re-signified in relation to other bodies.[8]

I mostly consider this oscillating movement to be invisible to other people's eyes. However, in Crossfield's images it seems to gain partial visibility. Crossfield uses the fictional body as a tool to represent body-images of aging subjects in a "reversed" mirror. His images present adult

---

8   I want to emphasize here that the speculative body is not necessarily experienced as a visual image, but rather as material presence.

subjects who embrace, rather than distance themselves from, the fantasy of the body in bits and pieces. As a consequence, the body-image of these individuals loses its unified appearance, spills over the borders of a "rectangular" mirror reflection, and merges with another subject's body. Moreover, it becomes fictional (through digitized mutation) and performative (through the enactment of a new form of self-seeing). The child's revolutionary differentiation between the *I* and the mother is disrupted, opening up the possibility for Crossfield's fantasy of exceedingly intimate, if not merged, selves and bodies.

MIRRORED INTIMACY

In "Fear of Intimacy," Cecilia Sjöholm argues for a revaluation of intimacy within psychoanalytic theory. She gives an account of the ways that intimacy is neglected or is given a negative connotation in Lacan's and Freud's theories. Their fear of or caution against intimacy is on the one hand historically linked to the Enlightenment ideal of separating the private from the public. The private sphere is related to the emotional and sensory aspects of life, and those are disregarded for being unstable, inconsistent, and vulnerable (Sjöholm 2009: 179). On the other hand, the intimate issues of sexuality are an important part of psychoanalytic therapy and are treated with care to avoid falling into an affective and emotional discourse (ibid: 179). Lacan's refusal of intimacy is born from the notion that the emotional inner life of the subject belongs to the imaginary, a sphere that psychoanalysis must traverse. In the space of psychoanalytic practice, the emergence of intimacy is thus not only assisted by the "confessional" discourse and the role of the couch, but it is also resisted in order to avoid reification of the unconscious (ibid: 179).

In his *Seminars* (1997 and 1998), Lacan introduces the term "extimacy" (*extimité*) or "intimate exteriority." The subject is intimately linked to that which is radically foreign and exterior to it. For Lacan, the Other is always exterior to the I, although, as he states, it is "at the heart of me" (1997: 71). Discussing the term, Jacques-Alain Miller writes:

Extimacy is not the contrary of intimacy. Extimacy says that the intimate is Other –
like a foreign body, a parasite. ... The extimacy of the Other is tied to the vacillation
of the subject's identity to himself. (1994: 76)

This understanding of the subject and her symbolic Other as tied to each
other by their intimate exteriority, and as constituted by what is strange
(*entfremdet*) yet familiar (*vertraut*), explains Lacan's reservation toward
intimacy as emotional attachment and uncontrolled reciprocity. Intimacy
does not exist without its potentially precarious counterpart; as I contend,
the subject does not exist without an (internalized) foreign body. The
Other, being at the heart of the subject, yet also exterior to the I, is
unassimilable and yet it mediates between the self and others (Evans 1996:
136). This Other appears for the first time in the infant's mirror image in
the Gestalt of the symbolic mother, who introduces the child to language
and the social order.

The mirror functions seemingly to put into practice Lacan's rejection of
intimacy as a way to relate to ourselves in relation to others. The autonomy
of the subject is at stake here, since intimacy requires openness to others
without total identification. I suggest that aging subjects may produce
positive body-images precisely through this openness to others, which
might break the dynamic of strong identification with the mirrored self.

Drawing on Julia Kristeva's reassessment of intimacy within
psychoanalysis, Sjöholm contends that "[a] discourse of intimacy does
nothing to revolutionize society, but it may well present us with a certain
protection against the colonization of ready-made images that marks the
capitalist society of aggressive new media" (192). I would like to fit
Sjöholm's "ready-made images" and "aggressive new media" into
Silverman's "dominant cultural screen." The disidentification with the
mirror image for aged subjects, as described by Freud, de Beauvoir, and
Woodward, seems to be conditioned on the discrepancy between a more or
less successful self-reflection in the mirror and the lack of a subject's
intimate relation to her corporeal self. This appears to create a split between
visuality and intimate corporeality. Yet I want to suggest that Crossfield
shows how the body can be conceptualized within the field of vision as an
intimate object, an object that allows for a relation to other bodies not only
on the basis of the autonomy of the subject formed in the mirror stage, but

also, and simultaneously, on the basis of a shared sense of self that is achieved through the disruption of this same autonomy by way of intimacy.

Hanneke Grootenboer proposes a theory of the intimacy of vision (2006) in relation to eye miniature portraits from the eighteenth century. Eye miniatures are portraits of a single eye of a beloved person, dead or alive, which are received as presents and worn on the body as precious ornaments. Grootenboer argues that the miniature's subject matter is intimate vision (497). The small paintings reverse the object and subject of seeing, and thus stand for a reciprocal mode of vision. Grootenboer's conception adds an important factor to the reciprocity theorized by Lacan's. The eye pictures are portrayals of a "sight," rather than a representation of a body part. As Grootenboer writes, "What they show is a mode of being seen, rather than of seeing, that has been withdrawn from representation only to recur in moments of self- reflexivity" (ibid: 505).

This observation ascribes a certain visual agency to the object, the image. In this view a form of intimacy, sensibility, and corporeality is attributed to the object. Is it possible for aging bodies to elicit a similar form of transformation in the order of vision? The openness to others involved in intimacy, and the intimacy of vision that is triggered by specific visual objects or, one might argue, by specific bodies, would then lead to a reconsideration of the importance of the mirror for the formation of identity.

To disidentify with the image in a physical mirror's frame as we age does not foreclose an identification with our reflected image in others.[9] As we lose the coherence of our self-image, we lose the mirror's complicity in self-identification, and we achieve identification through others, not radical, but intimate others. This body-image is related to its reflection in others' bodies rather than the mirror. Such a recognition allows for the idea of intimacy as something that combines the self's relation to her body and the physical contact or exchange with another's body.

Crossfield shows how the physical intimacy of his two older models allows them to engage lovingly vis-à-vis their reflection without the fatal effects of Ovid's Narcissus. The two subjects look and see each other reflected simultaneously. The duality of their bodies is stronger than the

---

9   See chapter 3 in the present book on Merleau-Ponty's concept of the "mirror in the flesh."

seductive power of the mirror: they hold each other, and they hold each other back from drowning in their reflection. The reflective surface strengthens the two subjects' intimate alliance by doubling it. Two bodies merge into one mass of limbs and flesh, and become a new form of self. They are neither quite one nor two, challenging the norm of an independent corporeal identity, permeating spatial, physical, and temporal confines. In Crossfield's *Narcissus,* the subject engages with his mirror-image such that self and self-image are separate, yet inseparable. One individual is distinguishable from the other, yet the borders between them are suspended. Their duality becomes a form of composite unity. Separation is shown as the condition for complex unification and vice versa. Intimacy is characterized as corporeal dialogue, shared vulnerability, the inhabiting of transparent boundaries, and reciprocal identification. And intimacy is made visible and tangible through the presence, yet not the power, of the mirror. Here, it is not the mirror that frames the subject, but the subjects themselves who, together, frame their reflections.

To take a further step, I would like to turn to a sculpture by American artist Robert Gober (*Untitled*, 1990; Fig. 14). A waxy, sack-like torso, with breasts, hair, a navel, wrinkles, and creases, stands on the floor, biding its time. The material's surface has a warm quality, although the pale color makes the texture seem cold. The torso embodies two anatomically contrasting sides, divided by a hairline that marks the center: a fleshy, smooth female breast and a flat, hairy male chest. The two sides show male and female body parts on a figure otherwise sexless. Missing a head, arms, shoulders, and lower body, the sculpture does not show primary sexual characteristics. Clear male or female markers like genitals, facial expressions, muscle, fat distribution, hair-growth, bone-structure, or posture are all omitted. While the trunk on the whole looks stiff, the right breast seems alive, plump with blood and fat tissue, slightly weighing down the right side of the body. The folds of skin are thick and firm, and remind the viewer as much of human flesh as of creases in a cement-filled paper bag. All in all, the trunk embodies indefinable states of age, sex, health, and aliveness. The sculpture exudes a mixture of helplessness (as subject) and uselessness (as object). It combines the disparate qualities of life and death, subjectivity and objecthood, agency and docility.

Unlike *Narcissus*, it molds two separate corporeal shapes within a single body. The sculpted body takes the form of a mirror of sorts. It emphasizes the vertical symmetry of human bodies, not by replicating it, but precisely by refusing the supposed reflection or likeness of the body's left and right sides. Like Crossfield's photograph, this artwork too seems to rob the mirror of its function as the necessary counterpart for subject formation, and so allows for a new definition of body-image. Additionally, Gober's torso consists of more than one, yet not quite two, subjects, who share one body. Physical intimacy is transposed from two subjects to one body. If, in Crossfield's work, the subjects' intimacy is partly expressed by their shared look into the mirror, Gober's sculpture abstains from the intimate look, even as it attracts the viewer through the torso's appealing as well as disturbing fleshiness.

My point about the mirror is that it brings to the fore the subject's exteriority, constituted by and intimately linked to others' bodies. Crossfield and Gober visualize this exteriority by showing two bodies folded into one. To develop my argument further and to bring it closer to my central topic of aging bodies, here I introduce a photographic self-portrait by American artist John Coplans (*Back with Arms above*, 1984; Fig. 15). This image reveals a singular body; yet, if we consider it through the lens of the reverse mirror stage, it projects an alternative to the uncanny recognition of a subject's aged self in the mirror.

The square backside reminds us of the form of a mirror while presenting us with the body's reverse side. Coplans's aged, hairy, and freckled backside does not reveal the characteristic outline of a body whereby the viewer could attach an identity to the subject. Thus, the title of the work is confusing. The parenthetical addition, "(*Back with Arms above*)," suggests that the self of the artist is either expressed through only minimal references to his body and posture, or, alternately, is inexpressible in a picture to begin with. The lack of personalizing features may indicate that the artist questions the capacity of an image to be a representative portrait of a self or body. Although one might identify this body as male, gender has become meaningless. The image does not contain or expose a self, but reflects on the concept of portraying a self. The work uses the visual object through which a self is commonly represented, the body, yet it displays it in such a way that it mocks the identificatory effect of corporeal depiction.

Fig. 14: Untitled

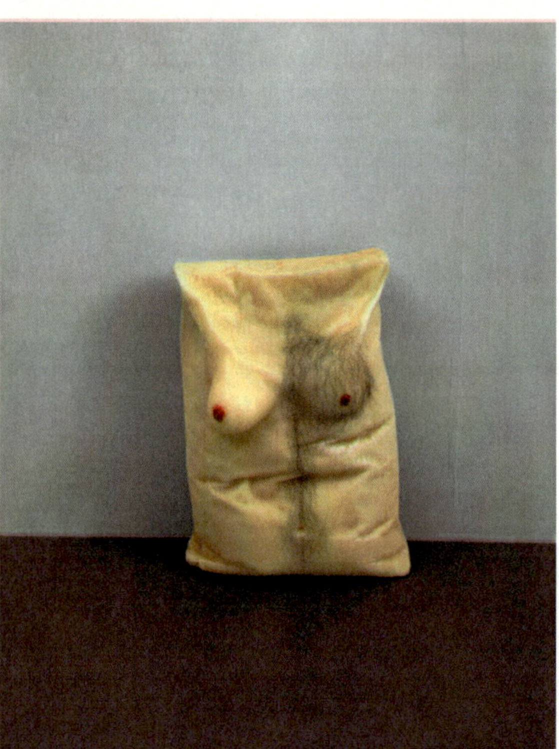

Source: Robert Gober (1990), © Collection of the artist

Coplans's back displays a mirror in the flesh. Reversing the traditional perspective of a body, the work depicts a blind yet living mirror. The two fists on top of the back have replaced the missing head. They seem almost aggressively directed toward the viewer, as if to say, "Return your gaze to yourself, I will not serve as your mirror." One might imagine the sitter's head to be turned inwards, toward the breast, toward the intimate self that is protected by the angled arms, hidden from view. Here, intimacy can be interpreted as a form of self-protection from vision and as indifference to the mirror. Coplans's hidden eyes are thus not blind, but look *within* the body for identification. The reversed torso shows us its inverted gaze and so depicts a "mirror within." In my view, the photograph offers a literal portrayal of a reversed mirror stage in old age, bringing to the fore a form of intimacy of the subject with his own body.

Fig. 15: Self-Portrait (Back with Arms above)

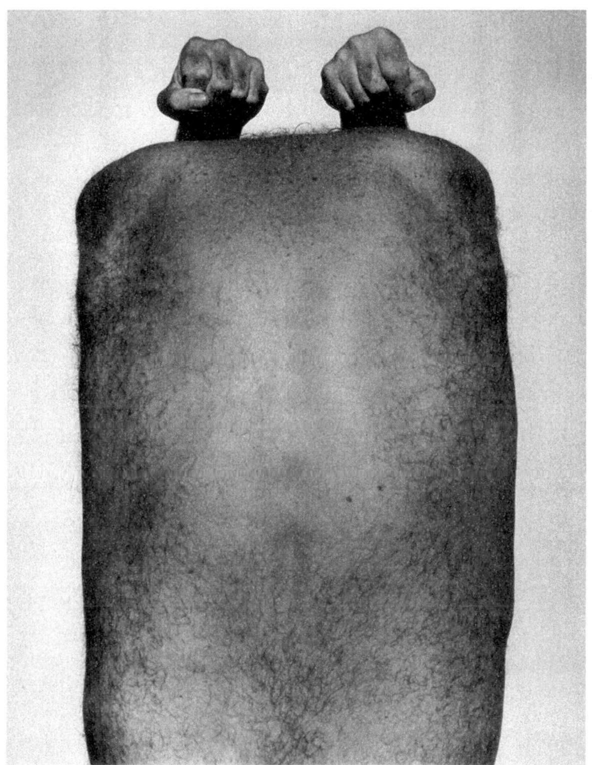

Source: John Coplans (1984), © Tate London & The John Coplans Trust

Coplans reverses the direction of the look onto his body, from without to within, from upright to upside-down. The change of visual direction allows him to redefine his body-image. In Coplans's photograph, the verticality of the symbolized mirror in the flesh is still intact. In a different way, I see the mirror's rotation from vertical to horizontal in Crossfield's image as a changing of visual direction with an even stronger redefining effect.

HORIZONTALITY AND THE *INFORME*

In Crossfield's *Narcissus*, the bodies' position, the puddle, and the mirror image all oppose the vertical axis that is constitutive of Lacan's mirror scene. Lacan accepts the psychologists' term "good form" to describe the infant's first discovery of a figure of wholeness, coherence and balance, which prefigures the "I" (Krauss 1997: 89). As Rosalind Krauss observes, Lacan does not mention that this

image, as seen in the mirror, will also be upright. ... All images – whether seen on a horizontal plane or not – will enter the space of his or her imagination as upright: aligned with the verticality of that viewer's body. (ibid: 90)

In contrast, Crossfield's photograph stresses the horizontal plane: all the horizontal lines in the image and of the picture as a whole are longer than their vertical counterparts. The room's walls are cut low, giving the room an elongated appearance; the rusted heater is more wide than tall, despite its vertical rungs; the two bodies as well as the pool on the floor have sprawled and splattered in such a way that makes it impossible to see a clear geometrical configuration. In this way, horizontality and a certain formlessness come together.

The ideal form-giving mirror is laid down, and the (self-)representation of the two men is instantly transformed. The unity achieved by the mirror is shattered. The figures' joint form and their selves' formation are recast along the horizontal plane of the supposedly animalistic and sexual field of perception.

With respect to Freud's interpretation of the function of man's "Gestalt" as "erecting himself from the earth" (2010: 66) and thus shifting his interest "away from the genitals on to the shape of the body as a whole," Krauss, drawing extensively on Georges Bataille, develops the concept of the "formless" (Krauss and Bois 1997: 91-92). To connect the concept of the formless to the cultural importance of form in relation to gender and other categorizations, I would like to refer to an artwork by the Romanian sculptor Constantin Brancusi.

Fig. 16: Torso of a Young Man I

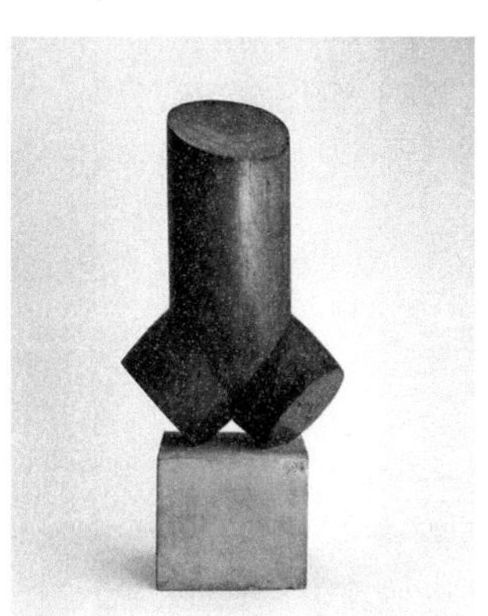

Source: Constantin Brancusi (1917-22), The Philadelphia Museum of Art, © Photo SCA-LA, Florence

Brancusi's *Torso of a Young Man I* (1917-22; Fig. 16) combines the symbol of a phallus and the concept of Gestalt. The strict verticality of the sculpture, the missing arms, the upper body's straight orientation, and the stone pedestal all cite the traditional form of a torso. Yet, the sculpture can be interpreted as a torso only because of the leg stumps at its bottom. The smooth wooden form does not allow the viewer to compare it to a human body. The allusion to an erect penis is the sole ground that entails such a comparison. Paradoxically, what makes Brancusi's torso look like a torso is its semblance to a fantasmatic penis. The sculpture's excessively articulated use of structure and shape plays with the replacement of one form with another. The form of the penis represents and replaces the implication of a torso.

Thus, Brancusi seems to have used the concept of the formless in a distinct way. He presents the viewer with the strongest symbol for sexual difference and power, which, after Freud and Lacan, also marks the simultaneous superiority and fragility of the human subject. The relation between Gestalt and verticality is exceedingly evident here, a fact all the more significant in the case of Lacan's theory of the mirror stage and its implicit phallic dimension put forth almost forty years after Brancusi created his sculpture. If a torso, a part of the body that represents less of a subject than the head or face, is shaped in the form of a penis, it implicates a peculiar link to the formation of subjectivity. The phallic impression is intensified by the extreme verticality of the sculpture. Of course, if it actually represented an erect penis, the sculpture would have to be more or less horizontal. The longest of the three cylinders that represents the upper body points upwards in such a rigid way that the two shorter tubes, representing leg stumps while alluding to testicles, appear to be pulled outward involuntarily. Hence, the figure looks like the reverse of a limp penis pulled downwards by gravity. Although the phallic form is an evident and necessary element lending the sculpture the appearance of a torso, Brancusi's art object transforms form. Form is here used in a way that links the body to subjecthood through sexual difference.

Fig. 17: Torso of a Young Girl II

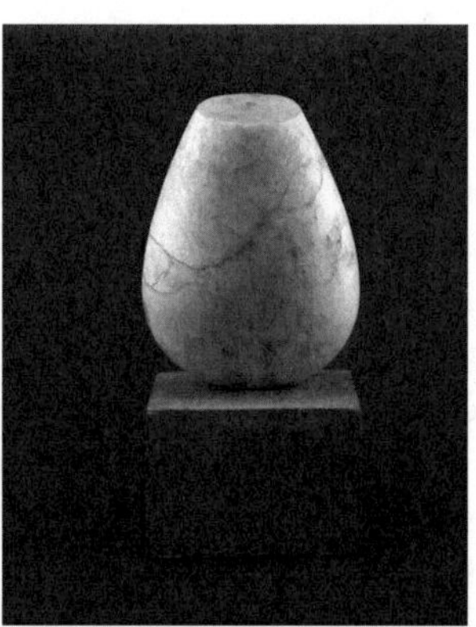

Source: Constantin Brancusi (1923), The Philadelphia Museum of Art,© Photo SCA- LA, Florence

This link is also visible in Brancusi's *Torso of a Young Girl II* (1923; Fig. 17). This sculpture consists of one rounded piece of stone, pointed at the top, broader at the bottom and slightly leaning forward. The sculpture is made of pink marble, showing the stone's fissures that look like veins. The girl's torso, in contrast to the young man's, is merely an abstracted form of an upper body without arms and legs. As much as this sculpture could represent a man's body, the lack of the phallic form seems to dictate the marble's sex as female. Clear form, be it transformed or markedly absent, dictates the representational content of Brancusi's sculptures.

In contrast to Brancusi, Crossfield plays with the dissolution of clear forms without embracing the concept of anti-form. He thereby suspends the borders between bodies without losing the concept of the corporeal basis of subjectivity. Formlessness here does not refer to the opposite or negation of embodied form, but to its malleability. The subjects in Crossfield's images show an abundance of subjective energy directed toward each other or their viewers. Their challenged physical shapes do not remove their subjectivity. Their formlessness does not rob them of subjecthood; on the contrary, it awards them subject positions that expand beyond the frame of the small rectangular mirror of the ego-formation of each.

FORMLESS MATERIALITY

In Gober's wax sculpture, the formless takes on yet another quality. It is reminiscent of a particular stage in the process of casting metal or concrete sculptures. Like resin, but unlike plaster or concrete, wax is often used as a temporary mold in the casting of solid sculptures. In this sense, wax serves as a transient means of creating form. Gober's torso reverses the result and casts the temporary wax-figure as sculpture. The uncertainty of the material's texture and its lack of solidity suggests an ambiguity of form and content. The torso takes shape in the wax cast, but it does not acquire the stability of metal, concrete, or stone, frequently the final stage of creating an (art) object.

The wax-sack is the reverse trace of an object: it exists *before* the actual object, yet does not, as expected, disintegrate or dissolve *after* it. The pale "body bag" has form, but it conceptualizes the substance of bodies as being inherently formless. Two sides, left and right, female and male, can stay apart only with great effort. The contours of either sex are still partly visible, but dissolve in the sculpture as a whole. The distinctions between male and female, body and bag, shapeless wax and erect Gestalt, youth and old age, form and content break down in Gober's sculpture. The sculpture seems to resist and simultaneously amalgamate with the floor and walls against which it is placed. The figure's sagging appearance on the right side, seemingly caused by the weight of the slumping female breast, contradicts the sculpture's vertical position. Thus, Gober's art object erodes the distinction between figure and ground, and between form and shapelessness, by confusing structure and texture, or form and content.

Fig. 18: Nude

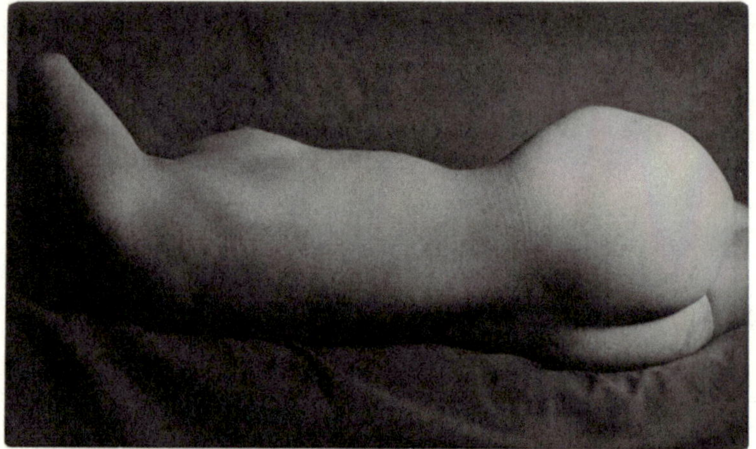

Source: Gyula Halasz Brassaï (1931-34), The Metropolitan Museum of Art

Brassaï's *Nude* (1931-34; Fig. 18) exposes a similar confusion of form through its play with the body's horizontality. The image shows a woman's torso lying on velvet drapery. The viewer is presented with the body's back and right side. One arm hides the woman's head; her legs are invisible. The image reveals a flattened half-sight of one breast, the round shapes of her buttocks, and an angular protrusion of her hipbones. Displaying a reclining instead of a standing figure, this female torso seems to stand in stark opposition to Brancusi's male torso. Taking the phallic structure of Lacan's ego-formation into account, one might see *Nude* as symbolizing the social construction of "femaleness."

However, I want to suggest that here, akin to *Torso of a Young Man I*, the viewing axis of the body is rotated. If, in Brancusi's sculpture, the penis-like stature exaggerates the ideal of an erect penis and thus mocks the principle of verticality, Brassaï's female torso challenges the feminine stereotype of horizontal posture. Despite the horizontal orientation, the body's most visible outlines are vertical. The light skin of the woman's side is silhouetted like a hilly landscape against the dark background. In contrast, her flat spine in the foreground almost disappears in the shadow. The vertical contours of the hipbone and arm are so prominent that at first sight the lying torso looks like a picture of a misty mountain range. Or, as Krauss observes in this image "rotation transmutes the female torso into phallus" (Krauss and Bois 1997: 157).[10]

Despite the opposed alignment of Brassaï's and Brancusi's torsos, both works alter the body's relation to form and formlessness. The interplay between visual and other perceptions of the body relates these two earlier, modernist works to the works of Crossfield and Gober. Crossfield's *Narcissus* can be compared to Brassaï's *Nude*; Gober's torso to Brancusi's. Yet, in contrast to the later art works, the bodies of Brassaï and Brancusi are cold, lifeless, distant, and inhuman. Not only do they blur distinctions between the sexes, but they also lack personality, age, warmth, and intimacy. Selfless and thus exchangeable, neither seems to have an identity. They are mere pictorial representations of bodies, despite their challenge to visual stereotypes.

In contrast, another sculpture by Gober, *Untitled* (1999; Fig. 19), expresses the body's individual reaction to circumstance.

---

10 If I compare the woman's body in Brassaï's photograph with a landscape I do not mean to compare women's bodies with nature. The comparison here merely serves to highlight the paradoxical relationship between the horizontal position of the body *in* the image and the vertical visual impression *of* the image.

Fig. 19: Untitled

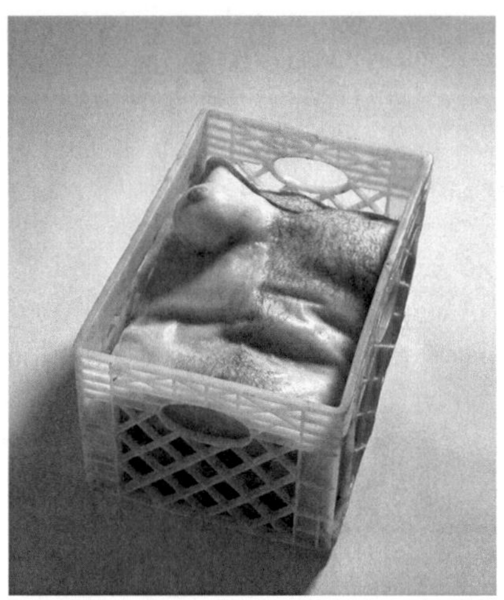

Source: Robert Gober (1999), © Collection
Walker Art Center

The same waxy female/male torso is now squeezed into a plastic crate, shedding all bodily characteristics in its being submitted to the rigorous form of its enclosure. The crate looks like the torso's prison; yet, at the same time, the body seems to snuggle itself comfortably into the container. Again, the discrepancy between constraining form and malleable content emphasizes their mutual dependency and inseparability. Entropy, as defined by Uros Cvoro, "eradicates the distances between binary oppositions such as form and content, thus contesting the production of meaning" (2002: 56). The body shows entropic characteristics insofar as it partially melds with its surrounding space. If we learn to see beyond the body's structural outlines, body-images could take form beyond the rectangle looking glass and inform our selves less restrictively after we have grown out of the mirror stage.

Lacan asks a crucial question: "We should like to know what the ego would be in a world in which no one had any idea of mirror symmetry" (Lacan in Krauss and Bois 1997: 170). [11] Krauss answers: "Without

---

11 In Krauss's book on the Formless she does not give a reference for Lacan's statement. But in a different essay (Krauss 1966: 44) she refers the reader to p.

consciousness of 'mirror symmetry' the subject would dissolve into space, and the world, anthropocentric for the Gestalt-oriented human, would be stripped of its qualities, made characterless, isotropic" (ibid: 171). I want to contend, however, that as much as Gober's and Crossfield's works dissolve their subjects into space, they do not make them characterless. Rather, the loss of symmetry breaks the spell of the mirror and returns the power of self-identification to subjects beyond infancy.

Mirroring aging bodies in a productive way entails breaking the mirror's spell and transforming its identificatory powers. It involves expanding the mirror's scope and transmitting its promises to other objects and embodied subjects. Crossfield's and Gober's art works provoke such a rupture in the limited yet effective charm of the looking glass. In pointing to the fissures, rough edges, blind spots, and potential failures of the mirror, in treating it as a fallible object, while conceptualizing it as a form of intimate substance, I have aimed to expose self-formation, especially for aging subjects, as a process in which one not only relies on the mirror, but must also be suspicious of it, and possibly resist its lure.

---

77 in Lacan's essay "De nos antécédents" in *Ecrits* (Paris: Editions du Seuil, 1966).

Afterword

Die Praxis der Ästhetik zeigt sich als kaleidoskopische Logik, welche die Materialität einzelner Darstellungsmöglichkeiten und ihre Anordnung als ein Nebeneinander erprobt. Nicht als Gegenmodell zu Verkörperung, sondern als Komplement dazu erforscht sie neue Körper durch Entkörperung der eigenen Methoden und eröffnet somit viele unterschiedliche Bühnen der Reflexion.

GESA ZIEMER

If art as process, in the exhibition of it, is … a cellular community—where, as in an organism, differentiation happens—then each cell requires the willingness of its environment (its viewers) to be absorbed into its ever-extending multiplicity.

MIEKE BAL

Entering the exhibition space, the viewer encounters an oval-shaped cage made of steel wire (Fig. 20). Its door is closed, suggesting we are not invited to enter the encircled space except through visual means. Within the cage are a white petticoat and an oversized dressing-table mirror that reflects a stuffed, human-sized cloth figure, hanging in mid-air, suspended from the ceiling.

Fig. 20: Cell XXVI

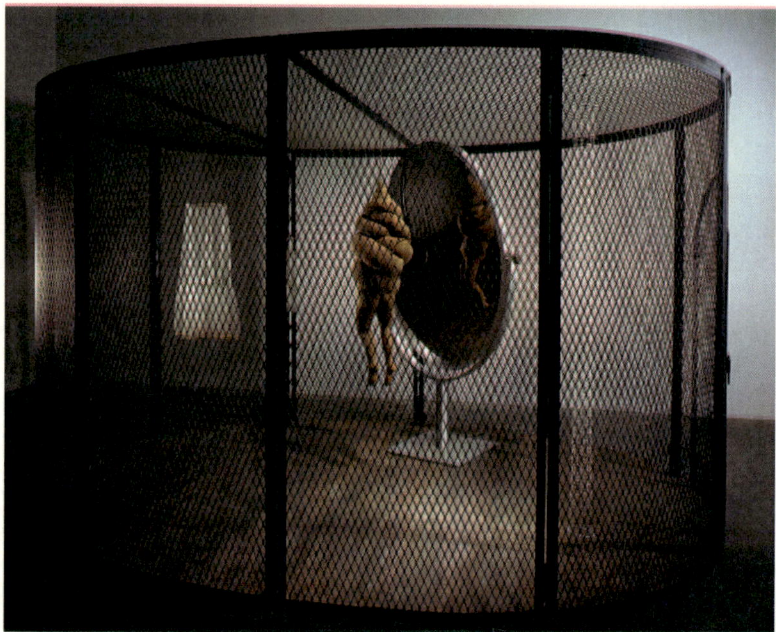

Source: Louise Bourgeois (2003), Gemeentemuseum Den Haag

The doll-like sculpture looks like a stylized piece of dog-poo, with legs sticking out. The twirled upper part hampers the recognition of human features, but the lower part's extremities suggest a likeness to the human body. This artwork by Louise Bourgeois not only helps to flesh out some of the concepts I have worked with and through in this study, but also allows me to project a look forward, toward unthought thoughts and unknown theories that might allow us to take a more creative look at our bodies and our selves.

The skirt, the mirror, and the body within the cell's enclosure are taken in by the viewer's look, though they seem to be unrelated to the viewer. And yet it is through this apparent indifference to the spectator that they become involved with each other, and so become capable of symbolically leaving the confined space. The three objects are at first sight unconnected, but have in common their joint presence in the steel cell – in sharp contrast to the viewer, who is locked out. A small round hole in the wire fence instinctively draws the viewer to come closer and peep inside, where she to some extent shares visually the confidential space of the caged objects, while remaining physically banned.

The viewer is thus simultaneously excluded and included in the artwork. We experience here a form of intimacy that does not build on a clear distinction between closeness and distance; this intimacy is created by a wavering between what seem to be spatial and corporeal opposites. Detachment becomes part of the intimate encounter with the cell's interior; the viewer as well as the confined objects can renegotiate their relationality beyond the conditions imposed by dichotomous restrictions.

This alienated form of intimacy between viewer and artwork reflects my attempt to take notions of autonomous subjecthood and the subject-object opposition and make them more complex. It also indicates my perspective on visuality as exposed to and partially disabled by the unknown, the impossible, the unlikely. In Bourgeois's *Cell*, the viewer confronts the impossibility of seeing herself in the huge mirror that hangs within the cell. The looking-glass is positioned in such a way that someone who is standing outside the cell cannot find herself reflected in it. Thus, this mirror not only exposes the mirror's blind spot – which is to say, the improbable likelihood that the seeing subject will be produced visually – but also doubles and reinforces the presence of the objects in the cell. This mirror disturbs the causal relationship between visual and physical forms of appearance. Through the viewer's active gaze into the interior of the cell and her experience of standing outside the mirror's reflective scope, her physical presence, and its visual manifestation, are constrained. Hence, alternative modes of seeing and being are called for. The cell exhibits a form of simultaneous visual breakdown and bodily failure. Such a double failure has triggered my exploration of unknown forms of embodiment in relation to visuality.

In Bourgeois's *Cell XXVI*, the body occupies various positions: it takes the forms of absence (the empty petticoat, the un-mirrored viewer) and of presence (the doll, a visually active viewer), and assumes the function of a medium (the mirror) that links the two seemingly antagonistic corporeal positions. The artwork also turns the concept of sculpture inside out. *Cell* incorporates the exhibition space into the exhibited work as part of the installation. The physical impenetrability of the cell as material object is countered by the immersion of the viewer in the sculpture's conceptual space. Hence, the reading of the work as a whole, as well as of its elements, necessarily becomes an act of failure, because it denies the viewer a univocal standpoint vis-à-vis the installation's elements. As Mieke Bal contends in her analysis of Bourgeois's *Cell* series:

Countering as they do the translation of elements into words, works like the *Cells*, with their dense self-enclosure and complexly structured unity, insist on the failure of element-by-element translation for rendering or explaining the work as a whole. (2001:45)

The *Cell* does not only resist explanation as a whole, but it also resists being encountered as a whole: the viewer's body as well as the exhibitionary space are involved in the sculpture in such a way that they create their own blind spots. In other words, the viewer, becoming part of the sculpture's conceptual "body," occupies a point of view *within* the *Cell*'s outer dimensions and thus can only ever experience partial vision. The borders between inside and outside are shattered. Bourgeois's artwork not only invokes one meaning of *cell* – the smallest structural unit of a body – but also the sense of an "arresting" enclosure in which the viewer is captured.

Through this play of inside and outside, absence and presence, intimacy and distance, visibility and obscurity, the artwork exemplifies what has been the main aim of this study: to draw out and bring together, with the help of visual reflection, the human body's seemingly contradictory or exclusionary characteristics. I have reconsidered the effects and functions of allegedly negative concepts related to the body by mirroring them with their supposedly positive opposites. The mirror, metaphorically and literally, served as a means to disrupt oppositional fixity and polarity, commonly used to categorize human bodies. I alluded to features of the mirror that distort or blur rather than sharpen the reflected body images: blind spots; limited perspective; framed, arrested, and doubled vision; dazzling reflection; or color- and light-specific imaging. With reference to such visual "handicaps," I have wanted to point to the body's constant exposure to visual constraints and distortions, which figure so strongly in everyday images of our bodies that they have become invisible, but remain representative of cultural norms. I have traced ways of seeing in the scope of what Judith Halberstam describes as "the dark landscape of confusion, loneliness, alienation, impossibility, and awkwardness" (2011: 97); a scope deployed by critical art, queer art, and art that is as offline and thought-provoking as the theories of the body that I have tried to develop here.

My comments on Bourgeois's *Cell XXVI* conclude this project by reflecting on the paradoxical nature of the "cell." As prototype of life, the smallest yet indispensable functional unit of the living organism, the cell signifies the vital necessity as well as practical invisibility and unintelligibility of corporeal reality. The cell reveals the synthesis of contradictory characteristics as one of the conditions of life. Cellular growth increases the size of cells only provisionally until they split in two and double their number, becoming more numerous instead of bigger. This "mirroring" way of growing is the condition for an organism's survival, yet can also lead to death, if the cell division occurs uncontrollably. Such precarity of life, constituted by the very condition of living being, for me symbolizes the paradoxical character of concepts, theories, physical states, and affects that inform our lives and that make them simultaneously enjoyable, vulnerable, purposeful, and unstable. Bourgeois's *Cell* and the artworks discussed in this study bring out the complexity of life by pointing to the negative sides of positive qualities of our existence. However, they do not embrace or even celebrate negativity. Instead, they engage negativity to bring out the productive aspects of living with and through failure.

In the end, I see this double-edged quality, in which the negative and the positive lose their oppositional meanings and merge, as the premise for a life worth living. I would add that this quality is also the promise of the thematic of failure: as losers in the struggle to achieve coherence, self-sufficiency, success, efficiency, smoothness, perfection, competence, and legibility, "failing bodies" have the capacity to seek out and possibly build new forms of desirable lives. In this study, failure is conceptualized as an engagement with and a finding of comfort in shifting grounds, obscure vision, oblique angles, imperfections, dancing tables (Ahmed 2006: 164), and in the art of unbecoming (Halberstam 2011: 88). My aim has been to "de-script" bodies (*ent-schreiben*) rather than to describe them (*be-schreiben*), to disentangle them from normatively descriptive images, and to complicate simplified visions of our bodies. Bodies we fail are bodies we might ultimately learn to love.

Bibliography

Ahmed, Sara (2006): *Queer Phenomenology: Orientations, Objects, Others*, Durham, NC: Duke University Press.

Allen, Carolyn (1993): "The Erotics of Nora's Narrative in Djuna Barnes's *Nightwood*." In: *Signs* 19/1, pp. 177-200.

Althusser, Louis (1971 [1970]): "Ideology and Ideological State Apparatuses." In: *Lenin and Philosophy*, trans. by Ben Brewster, New York: Monthly Review Press, pp. 127-86.

Armstrong, David (1995): "The Rise of Surveillance Medicine." In: *Sociology of Health & Illness* 17/3, pp. 393-404.

Auslander, Philip/Sandahl, Carrie (2005): *Bodies in Commotion: Disability & Performance*, Ann Arbor: University of Michigan Press.

Austin, J. L. (2001 [1955]): *How To Do Things With Words*, Cambridge, MA: Harvard University Press.

Bal, Mieke (1996): *Double Exposures: The Subject of Cultural Analysis*, London: Routledge.

Bal, Mieke (1997): *Narratology. Introduction to the Theory of Narrative*, 2nd edition, Toronto: University of Toronto Press.

Bal, Mieke (1999a): *Quoting Caravaggio: Contemporary Art, Preposterous History*, Chicago: University of Chicago Press.

Bal, Mieke (2001): *Louise Bourgeois' Spider. The Architecture of Art Writing*, Chicago: University of Chicago Press.

Bal, Mieke (1999b): "Introduction." In: Mieke Bal and Hent de Vries (eds.), *The Practice of Cultural Analysis. Exposing Interdisciplinary Interpretation*, Stanford, CA: Stanford University Press, pp. 1-14.

Bal, Mieke (2005): "The Commitment to Look." In: *Journal of Visual Culture* 4/2, pp. 145-62.

Bal, Mieke (2006): "Exposing the Public." In: Sharon Macdonald (ed.), *A Companion to Museum Studies*, Oxford: Blackwell, pp. 525-42.

Bal, Mieke/Bryson, Norman (2001): *Looking In: The Art of Viewing*, London: Routledge.

Barnes, Djuna (2001 [1936]): *Nightwood*, London: Faber and Faber.

Barthes, Roland (1977): *Image – Music – Text*, London: Fontana Press.

Barthes, Roland (1982): *Camera Lucida. Reflections on Photography*, trans. by Richard Howard, New York: Hill and Wang, 1982.

Bann, Stephen (1989): *The True Vine: On Visual Representation and the Western Tradition*, Cambridge, UK: Cambridge University Press, 1989.

Batchen, Geoffrey (1999): *Burning with Desire: The Conception of Photography*, Cambridge, MA: MIT Press.

Beauvoir, Simone de (1996 [*La veillesse*, 1970]): *The Coming of Age*, trans. by Patrick O'Brian, New York: Norton.

Belting, Hans (2000): *Menschenbild und Körperbild*, Münster: Rhema.

Belting, Hans (2005): "Image, Medium, Body: A New Approach to Iconology." In: *Critical Inquiry* 31/ 2, pp. 302-19.

Benjamin, Walter (1979 [1931]): "A Small History of Photography." In: *One-Way Street and Other Writings*, London: New Left Books, pp. 240-57.

Betterton, Rosemary (2006): "Promising Monsters: Pregnant Bodies, Artistic Subjectivity, and Maternal Imagination." In: *Hypatia* 21/1, pp. 80-100.

Billeter, Erika, ed. (1985): *Self-Portrait in the Age of Photography: Photographers Reflecting Their Own Image*, Bern: Benteli.

Birrell, Susan/Cole, C. L., eds. (1994): *Women, Sport, and Culture*, Champaign, IL: Human Kinetics Publishers.

Bland, Lucy/Doane, Laura Doane, eds. (1998): *Sexology in Culture: Labelling Bodies and Desires*, Chicago: University of Chicago Press.

Bleeker, Maaike (2008a): *Visuality in the Theatre: The Locus of Looking.* New York: Palgrave Macmillan.

Bleeker, Maaike (2000): "Do You See What I Mean? Artifact and the Genesis of Vision on Stage." In: *Revue Internationale de Sémiotique Visuelle* 5, pp. 41-55.

Bleeker, Maaike (2008b): "Passages in Post-Modern Theory: Mapping the Apparatus." In: *Parallax* 14/1, pp. 55-67.

Blyn, Robin (2000): "From Stage to Page: Franz Kafka, Djuna Barnes, and Modernism's Freak Fictions." In: *Narrative* 8, pp. 134-59.

Blossfeldt, Karl (2006): *Urformen der Kunst: Wundergarten der Natur*, Munich: Schirmer/Mosel.

Boler, Megan (1997): "The Risks of Empathy: Interrogating Multiculturalism's Gaze." In: *Cultural Studies* 11/2, pp. 253-73.

Bourgeois, Louise (1998): *Destruction of the Father. Reconstruction of the Father: Writings and Interviews 1923-1997*, Cambridge, MA: MIT Press.

Bowie, Malcolm (1991): *Lacan.* Cambridge, MA: MIT Press.

Bright, Deborah, ed. (1998): *The Passionate Camera: Photography and Bodies of Desire*, New York: Routledge.

Bronfen, Elisabeth (1992): *Over Her Dead Body: Death, Femininity and the Aesthetic,* Manchester, UK: Manchester University Press.

Bryson, Norman (1983): *Vision and Painting· The Logic of the Gaze,* London: Macmillan.

Bryson, Norman (1998): "The Gaze in the Expanded Field." In: *Vision and Visuality*, Seattle: Bay Press, pp. 87-114.

Butler, Judith (1990): *Gender Trouble: Feminism and the Subversion of Identity*, New York: Routledge.

Butler, Judith (1993): *Bodies That Matter: On the Discursive Limits of "Sex,"* New York: Routledge.

Butler, Judith (1997): *Excitable Speech: A Politics of the Performative*, New York: Routledge.

Butler, Judith (2005): *Giving an Account of Oneself*, New York: Fordham University Press, 2005.

Butler, Judith (2006): *Precarious Life. The Powers of Mourning and Violence*, London: Verso, 2006.

Butler, Judith (1988): "Performative Acts and Gender Constitution: An Essay in Phenomenology and Feminist Theory." In: *Theatre Journal* 40, pp. 519-31.

Butler, Judith (2001): "Giving an Account of Oneself." In: *Diacritics* 31/4, pp. 22-40.

Butler, Judith (2003): "Afterword: After Loss, What Then?" In: D. Eng and D. Kazanjian (eds.), *Loss: The Politics of Mourning*, Berkeley: University of California Press, 467-74.

Cohler, Deborah (2010): *Citizen, Invert, Queer: Lesbianism and War in Early Twentieth-Century Britain*, Minneapolis: University of Minnesota Press.

Cristofovici, Anca (2009): *Touching Surfaces: Photographic Aesthetics, Temporality, Aging,* Amsterdam: Rodopi.

Crone, Rainer/Schaesberg, Petrus Graf (1998): *Louise Bourgeois: The Secret of the Cells*, Munich: Prestel.

Cvoro, Uros (2002). "The Present Body, the Absent Body, and the Formless." In: *Art Journal* 61/4, pp. 54-63.

Davis, Lennard J. (1999): "Crips Strike Back: The Rise of Disability Studies." In: *American Literary History* 11/3: 500-512.

Davis, Lennard J./Smith, Marquard (2006): "Editorial: Disability-Visuality." In: *Journal of Visual Culture* 5/2, pp. 131-36.

Deleuze, Gilles (1986): *Cinema 1: The Movement Image*, London, Continuum.

Deleuze, Gilles/Guattari, Félix (2004): *A Thousand Plateaus: Capitalism and Schizophrenia*, London: Continuum.

De Man, Paul (1979): "Autobiography as De-Facement." In: *MLN* 94/5, pp. 919-30.

Didi-Huberman, Georges (1992): *Ce que nous voyons, ce qui nous regarde*, Paris: Minuit.

Dillon, Sheila (2006): *Ancient Greek Portrait Sculpture: Contexts, Subjects, and Styles*, Cambridge UK: Cambridge University Press.

Doy, Gen (2004): *Picturing the Self: Changing Views of the Subject in Visual Culture,* London: I. B .Tauris.

Dyer, Richard (1997): *White*, London: Routledge.

Elkins, James (1996): *The Object Stares Back: On the Nature of Seeing*, New York: Simon & Schuster.

Elkins, James (1999): *Pictures of the Body. Pain and Metamorphosis*, Stanford: Stanford University Press.

Elkins, James (2008): *Six Stories from the End of Representation: Images in Painting, Photography, Astronomy, Microscopy, Particle Physics, and Quantum Mechanics, 1980-2000*, Stanford: Stanford University Press.

Ellis, Havelock (2007 [1927]): "Sexual Inversion." In: *Studies in the Psychology of Sex. Vol. II*, Middlesex, UK: The Echo Library.

Erikson, Erik H. (1972): *Insight and Responsibility: Lectures on the Ethical Implications of Psychoanalytical Insight*, London: Norton.

Evans, Dylan (1996): *An Introductory Dictionary of Lacanian Psychoanalysis*, London: Routledge.

Featherstone, Mike (1991): *The Body: Social Process and Cultural Theory*, London: Sage.

Foucault, Michel (1979 [1975]): *Discipline and Punish: The Birth of the Prison*, New York: Vintage.

Foucault, Michel (1990 [1976]): *The History of Sexuality. Volume 1: An Introduction*, New York: Vintage.

Foucault, Michel (1994 [1963]): *The Birth of the Clinic: An Archaeology of Medical Perception*, trans. by A. Sheridan, New York: Vintage.

Foucault, Michel (2003): *Die Anormalen. Vorlesungen am Collège de France (1974-75)*, Frankfurt am Main: Suhrkamp, 2003.

Fraser, Kathryn (1998): "The Photographic Insane." In: *Cinémas* 9/1, pp. 139-51.

Freud, Sigmund (1961 [1920]): *Beyond the Pleasure Principle*, New York: Norton.

Freud, Sigmund (1995 [1938]): *The Basic Writings of Sigmund Freud and Three Contributions to the Theory of Sex*, New York: Modern Library.

Freud, Sigmund (2000 [1905]): *Three Essays on the Theory of Sexuality*, trans. by James Strachey, New York: Basic.

Freud, Sigmund (2003 [1899-1919]): *The Uncanny*, trans. by David McLintock, London: Penguin, 2003.

Freud, Sigmund (2010 [1930]): *Civilization and Its Discontents*, Eastford, CT: Martino Publishing.

Freud, Sigmund (1989 [1914]): "On Narcissism: An Introduction." In: Peter Gay (ed.), *The Freud Reader*, New York: Norton.

Gage, John (1997): "Photographic Likeness." In: Joanna Woodall (ed.), *Portraiture: Facing the Subject*, Manchester, UK: Manchester University Press, pp. 119-30.

Gallagher, Jean (2001): "Vision and Inversion in *Nightwood*." *Modern Fiction Studies* 47/2, pp. 279-305.

Gallop, Jane (1987): *Reading Lacan*, Ithaca: Cornell University Press.

Gallop, Jane (1983): "Lacan's 'Mirror Stage': Where to Begin?" In: *SubStance* 11/4, pp. 118-28.

Garland-Thomson, Rosemary (2001): "Seeing the Disabled: Visual Rhetorics of Disability in Popular Photography." In: *The New Disability History: American Perspectives*. New York: NYU Press, pp. 335–74.

Garland-Thomson, Rosemary (2006): "Ways of Staring." In: *Journal of Visual Culture* 5/2, pp. 173-92.

Gilligan, Carol (1982): *In a Different Voice*, Cambridge, MA: Harvard University Press.

Grootenboer, Hanneke (2006): "Treasuring the Gaze: Eye Miniature Portraits and the Intimacy of Vision." In: *The Art Bulletin* 88/3, pp. 496-507.

Grootenboer, Hanneke (2010): "How to Become a Picture: Theatricality as Strategy in Seventeenth-Century Dutch Portraits." In: *Art History* 33/2, pp. 320-33.

Gullette, Margaret Morganroth (2004): *Aged by Culture*, Chicago: University of Chicago Press.

Halberstam, Judith (1995): *Skin Shows: Gothic Horror and the Technology of Monsters*, Durham, NC: Duke University Press, 1995.

Halberstam, Judith (2011): *The Queer Art of Failure*, Durham, NC: Duke University Press, 2011.

Halberstam, Judith (1993): "Technologies of Monstrosity: Bram Stoker's *Dracula*." In: *Victorian Studies* 36 (1993): 333-52.

Haraway, Donna (2004): *The Haraway Reader*, London: Routledge.

Hayles, Katherine (1999): *How We Became Posthuman: Virtual Bodies in Cybernetics, Literature and Informatics*, Chicago: University of Chicago Press.

Hirschfeld, Magnus (1991 [1910]): *Transvestites: The Erotic Drive to Cross-Dress*, Buffalo NY: Prometheus Books.

Holland, Sharon Patricia (2000a): *Raising the Dead: Readings of Death and (Black) Subjectivity*, Durham, NC: Duke University Press, 2000.

Holland, Sharon Patricia (2000b): "Queering Black Performance." In: *Callaloo* 23, pp. 384-93.

Johnson, Barbara (1982): "My Monster / My Self." In: *Diacritics* 12/2, pp. 2-10.

Jones, Amelia (1998): *Body Art. Performing the Subject*, Minneapolis: University of Minnesota Press.

Jones, Amelia (2002): "The 'Eternal Return': Self-Portrait as a Technology of Embodiment." In: *Signs: Journal of Women in Culture and Society* 27/4, pp. 947-78.

Kittelmann, Udo/Kyllikki, Zacharias, eds. (2010): *Hans Bellmer, Louise Bourgeois: Double Sexus*, Berlin: Distanz.

Knafo, Danielle (2001): "Claude Cahun: The Third Sex." In: *Studies in Gender and Sexuality* 2/1, pp. 29-61.

Koehn, Daryl (1998): *Rethinking Feminist Ethics: Care, Trust and Empathy*, London: Routledge.

Kouwenhoven, Bill (2010): "Antony Crossfield: The Body in Question." In: *HotShoe* 163, pp. 40-49.

Krafft-Ebing, Richard. (2011 [1886]): *Psychopathia Sexualis: The Classic Study of Deviant Sex*, trans. by Franklin S. Klaf, New York: Arcade Publishing.

Krauss, Rosalind E. (2000): *Bachelors*, Cambridge, MA: MIT Press.

Krauss, Rosalind E./Bois, Yve-Alain (1997): *Formless: A User's Guide*, New York: Zone.

Krauss, Rosalind E./Bois, Yve-Alain (1996): "A User's Guide to Entropy." In: *October* 78, pp. 38-88.

Kuppers, Petra (2003): *Disability and Contemporary Performance: Bodies on Edge*. London: Routledge.

Lacan, Jaques (1966): *Écrits*. Paris: Éditions du Seuil.

Lacan, Jacques (1968): *The Language of the Self*, trans. by Anthony Wilden, New York: Delta.

Lacan, Jacques (1997): *The Ethics of Psychoanalysis: 1959-1960*, ed. by Jacques-Alain Miller, New York: Norton.

Lacan, Jacques (1998 [1978]): *The Four Fundamental Concepts of Psychoanalysis*, trans. by Alan Sheridan, ed. by Jacques-Alain Miller, New York: Norton.

Lacan, Jacques (2006): *Ecrits: The First Complete Edition in English*, trans. by Bruce Fink, New York: Norton.

Lacan, Jacques (1953): "Some Reflections on the Ego." In: *International Journal of Psychoanalysis* 34, pp. 11-17.

Laplanche, Jean/Pontalis, Jean-Bertrand (1988): *The Language of Psycho-Analysis*, London: Karnac.

Latimer, T. T. (2006): "Entre Nous: Between Claude Cahun and Marcel Moore." In: *GLQ: A Journal of Lesbian and Gay Studies* 12/2, pp. 197-216.

Leder, Drew (1990): *The Absent Body*, Chicago: University of Chicago Press.

Levin, David Michael (1991): "Visions of Narcissism: Intersubjectivity and the Reversals of Reflection." In: M. C. Dillon (ed.) ,*Merleau-Ponty Vivant*, Albany: State University of New York Press, pp. 47-90.

Mapplethorpe, Robert (1986): *Black Book*, New York: St. Martin's.

Maxwell, Anne (2010): *Picture Imperfect: Photography and Eugenics, 1870-1940*, Eastbourne (UK): Sussex Academic Press.

McKenzie, Jon (2001): *Perform or Else. From Discipline to Performance*, London: Routledge.

Mercer, Kobena (1991): "Looking for Trouble." In: *Transition* 51, pp. 184-97.

Mercer, Kobena/Julien, Isaac (1986): "True Confessions: A Discourse on Images of Black Male Sexuality." In: *The Film Art of Isaac Julien*, ed. by David Frankel, New York: Bard College.

Merleau-Ponty, Maurice (1968 [1964]): *The Visible and the Invisible*, trans. by Alphonso Lingis, Evanston, IL: Northwestern University Press.

Meskimmon, Marsha (1996): *The Art of Reflection: Women Artists' Self-Portraiture in the Twentieth Century*, New York: Columbia University Press.

Miller, Jacques-Alain (1994): "Extimacy." In: Mark Bracher et al. (ed.), *Lacanian Theory of Discourse: Subject, Structure, and Society*, New York: NYU Press, pp. 74-87.

Mitchell, W. J. T. (1992): *The Reconfigured Eye: Visual Truth in the Post-Photographic Era*, Cambridge, MA: MIT Press.

Mitchell, W. J. T. (2005): *What Do Pictures Want? The Lives and Loves of Images*, Chicago: University of Chicago Press.

Mitchell, W. J. T. (1984): "What Is an Image?" In: *New Literary History* 15/3, pp. 503-37.

Mitchell, W. J. T. (2001): "Seeing Disability." In: *Public Culture* 13/3, pp. 391-97.

Nancy, Jean-Luc (2002): *Hegel: The Restlessness of the Negative*, Minneapolis: University of Minnesota Press.

Nancy, Jean-Luc (1987): "Wild Laughter in the Throat of Death." In: *MLN* 102/4, pp. 719-36.

Nancy, Jean-Luc (2006): "The Look of the Portrait." In: *Multiple Arts: The Muses II*, Stanford: Stanford University Press.

Ovid (1994 [1916]): *Metamorphoses: Books 1-8*, trans. by Frank Justus Miller, Cambridge, UK: Cambridge University Press.

Panzanelli, Roberta, ed. (2008): *Ephemeral Bodies: Wax Sculpture and the Human Figure*, Los Angeles: Getty Publications, 2008.

Phelan, Peggy (1993): *Unmarked. The Politics of Performance*, London: Routledge.

Phelan, Peggy (1997): *Mourning Sex: Performing Public Memories*, London: Routledge.

Plath, Sylvia (2002 [1982]): *The Collected Poems*, London: Faber and Faber.

Pollock, Griselda (1990): "Introduction· Veils, Masks & Mirrors." In: *Correct Distance*, ed. by Mitra Tabrizian, Manchester, UK: Cornerhouse.

Price, Janet/Shildrick, Margrit, eds. (1999): *Feminist Theory and the Body*, New York: Routledge.

Prosser, Jay (2005): *Light in the Dark Room: Photography and Loss*, Minneapolis: University of Minnesota Press.

Prosser, Jay (2002): "A Palinode on Photography and the Transsexual Real." In: Nancy K. Miller and Jason Tougaw (eds.), *Extremities: Trauma, Testimony, and Community*, Urbana: University of Illinois Press.

Rajchman, John (1988): "Foucault's Art of Seeing." In: *October* 44, pp. 88–117.

Rank, Otto (1971 [1925]): *The Double: A Psychoanalytic Study*, trans. by H. Tucker, Jr., New York: New American Library.

Rice, Sedt/Gumpert, Ledt, eds. (1999): *Inverted Odysseys: Claude Cahun, Maya Deren, Cindy Sherman*, Cambridge, MA: MIT Press.

Robinson, Sally (2000): *Marked Men: White Masculinity in Crisis*, New York: Columbia University Press.

Rose, Jacqueline (2005): *Sexuality in the Field of Vision*, London: Verso.

Schmidt, Benjamin/Marius, Gesa Ziemer (2004): *Verletzbare Orte. Zur Ästhetik Anderer Körper auf der Bühne*, www.ith-z.ch, Zürich.

Sedgwick, Eve Kosofsky (2003): *Touching Feeling: Affect, Pedagogy, Performativity*, Durham, NC: Duke University Press, 2003.

Seitler, Dana (2001): "Down on All Fours: Atavistic Perversions and the Science of Desire from Frank Norris to Djuna Barnes." In: *American Literature* 73, pp. 525-62.

Seitler, Dana (2004): "Queer Physiognomies: Or, How Many Ways Can We Do the History of Sexuality?" In: *Criticism* 46/1, pp. 71-103.

Sekula, Alan (1986): "The Body and the Archive." In: *October* 39, pp. 3-64.

Shelley, Mary (1998 [1831]): *Frankenstein, or The Modern Prometheus*, Oxford, UK: Oxford University Press.

Shildrick, Margrit (2002): *Embodying the Monster. Encounters with the Vulnerable Self*, London: Sage.

Shildrick, Margrit (2000): "Becoming Vulnerable: Contagious Encounters and the Ethics of Risk." In: *Journal of Medical Humanities* 21/4, pp. 215-27.

Silk, Michael L./Andrew, David L./Cole, C. L., eds. (2005): *Sport and Corporate Nationalisms*, Oxford, UK: Berg.

Silverman, Kaja (1988a): *The Acoustic Mirror: The Female Voice in Psychoanalysis and Cinema*, Bloomington: Indiana University Press.

Silverman, Kaja (1992): *Male Subjectivity at the Margins*, London: Routledge.

Silverman, Kaja (1996): *The Threshold of the Visible World*, London: Routledge.

Silverman, Kaja (1988b): "Too Early/Too Late: Subjectivity and the Primal Scene in Henry James." In: *Novel: A Forum on Fiction* 21/2-3, pp. 147-73.

Singer, T. Benjamin (2006): "From the Medical Gaze to Sublime Mutations: The Ethics of (Re) Viewing Non-Normative Body Images." In: Stephen Whittle and Susan Stryker (eds.), *The Transgender Studies Reader*, London: Routledge, pp. 601-20.

Sjöholm, Cecilia (2009): "Fear of Intimacy? Psychoanalysis and the Resistance to Commodification." In: Kelly Oliver and S. K. Keltner (eds.), *Psychoanalysis, Aesthetics, and Politics in the Work of Julia Kristeva*, Albany: State University of New York Press, pp. 179-94.

Smalls, James (2006): *The Homoerotic Photography of Carl Van Vechten: Public Face, Private Thoughts*, Philadelphia: Temple University Press.

Snyder, Sharon L./Mitchell, David T. (2001): "Re-Engaging the Body: Disability Studies and the Resistance to Embodiment." In: *Public Culture* 13/3, pp. 367-89.

Sontag, Susan (2002 [1979]): *On Photography*, London: Penguin.

Sontag, Susan (1985): "Certain Mapplethorpes." In: Robert Mapplethorpe, *Certain People: A Book of Portraits*. Pasadena, CA: Twelvetree Press, 1985.

Stevenson, Robert Louis (1896 [1981]): *The Strange Case of Dr. Jekyll and Mr. Hyde*, New York: Bantam.

Stewart, Garrett (1990): *Reading Voices: Literature and the Phonotext*, Berkeley: University of California Press.

Stewart, Garrett (1987): "Photo-Gravure: Death, Photography, and Film Narrative." In: *Wide Angle* 9, pp. 11-31.

Stoker, Bram (1981 [1897]): *Dracula*, New York: Bantam.

Stryker, Susan/Whittle, Stephen, eds. (2006): *The Transgender Studies Reader*, New York: Routledge.

Tanner, Laura E. (2006): *Lost Bodies: Inhabiting the Borders of Life and Death*, Ithaca: Cornell University Press.

Taussig, Michael (1991): "Tactility and Distraction." In: *Cultural Anthropology* 6/2, pp. 147-53.

Tomkins, Silvan S. (1963): *Affect, Imagery, Consciousness: Volume II, The Negative Affects*, New York: Springer.

Van Alphen, Ernst (1993): *Francis Bacon and the Loss of Self*, Cambridge, MA: Harvard University Press.

Van Alphen, Ernst (2005): *Art in Mind: How Contemporary Images Shape Thought*, Chicago: University of Chicago Press.

Van Alphen, Ernst (1997): "The Portrait's Dispersal: Concepts of Representation and Subjectivity in Contemporary Portraiture." In Joanna Woodall (ed.), *Portraiture: Facing the Subject*, Manchester, UK: Manchester University Press, pp. 239–56.

Van Alphen, Ernst (1999): "Affective Reading. Loss of Self in Djuna Barnes' *Nightwood*." In: Mieke Bal and Hent de Vries (eds.): *The Practice of Cultural Analysis: Exposing Interdisciplinary Interpretation*, Stanford: Stanford University Press, pp. 151-70.

Van den Dries, Luk (2002): *Bodycheck: Relocating the Body in Contemporary Performing Art*, Amsterdam: Rodopi.

Wilde, Oscar (1981 [1891]): *The Picture of Dorian Gray*, Oxford: Oxford University Press.

Winnubst, Shannon (2004): "Is the Mirror Racist? Interrogating the Space of Whiteness." In: *Philosophy & Social Criticism* 30/1, pp. 25-50.

Wolf, Sylvia (2007): *Mapplethorpe: Polaroids*, Munich: Prestel.

Woodall, Joanna, ed. (1997): *Portraiture: Facing the Subject*, Manchester, UK: Manchester University Press.

Woodward, Kathleen (1999): *Figuring Age: Women, Bodies, Generations*, Bloomington: Indiana University Press.

Woodward, Kathleen (1983): "Instant Repulsion: Decrepitude, the Mirror Stage, and the Literary Imagination." In: *The Kenyon Review* 5/4, pp. 43-66.

Ziemer, Gesa (2008): *Verletzbare Orte: Entwurf einer praktischen Ästhetik*, Zürich: Diaphanes.